A GUIDE TO
MILITARY ART

BANDS, BANDSMEN
AND
SHEET MUSIC COVERS

# A GUIDE TO MILITARY ART

# BANDS, BANDSMEN AND SHEET MUSIC COVERS

by Ray Westlake

The Naval & Military Press

For '28 Up The Hill' – full of music everyday

© Ray Westlake 2021

*Published by*

**The Naval & Military Press Ltd**
Unit 5 Riverside
Bellbrook Industrial Estate
Uckfield, East Sussex
TN22 1QQ England

Tel: +44 (0) 1825 749494

**www.naval-military-press.com**

# CONTENTS

Acknowledgments . . . . . . . . . . . . . . . . . . . . . . viii

Introduction . . . . . . . . . . . . . . . . . . . . . . . . . . . ix

Section One – Bands and Bandsmen . . . . . . . . . . 1

Section Two – Sheet Music Covers . . . . . . . . . . . 37

Bibliography . . . . . . . . . . . . . . . . . . . . . . . . . . 51

# ACKNOWLEDGMENTS

I must, as always, acknowledge the help and encouragement given to me by my wonderful wife Claire. Also to Peter Harrington of the Anne SK Brown Military Collection, which is held at the Brown University Library, Providence Rhode Island, USA. I cannot thank the Collection enough for its generosity in allowing me to used many of the images in this book. Much is also always owed by an author to his publisher, in this case Chris and Gary Buckland of the Naval and Military Press.

# INTRODUCTION

It was film producer and pioneer of the American animation industry Walt Disney who said, 'Of all of our inventions for mass communication, pictures still speak the most universally understood language.' And, of course, we must not forget the wider usage of 'A picture is worth a thousand words.' Certainly, if we set out to make a study of uniform, we can learn much from looking at pictures. But, as that superb reference work published by the Army Museums Ogilby Trust in 1972, *Index To British Military Costume Prints 1500-1914*, points out, '…it must not be supposed that a contemporary artist, however celebrated, does not make mistakes in drawing what he thought he had seen.' To this we could add, 'or what he thought might look good'—artistic licence, in fact. Here, as an example, I bring to mind a comment made by none less than Richard Caton Woodville who, after the end of the Great War, was given a commission by the London Scottish to paint a picture recalling that regiment's brave stand at Messines Ridge at the end of October 1914. Up in the Mess went the finished article. Those who were there pointed out recognisable faces and features of the battle and in general were pleased at what they saw. But up stepped one veteran who, with finger pointing, exclaimed, 'They're wearing sporrans. We never had them on the Ridge. They were left behind at our billets.' This important uniform detail was raised later with the artist who remarked without hesitation, 'Yes, I'm quite aware of this. I included them as I thought the men looked quite empty without them.'

At this point the serious student of military dress may well abandon the idea of including prints and pictures in his study of the subject, and instead content him or herself with official publications such as Dress or Clothing Regulations. 'But, before the critic condemns an artist for depicting a uniform that was never approved under the regulations' (*Index to British Military Costume Prints* again) 'let him remember that the British officer has long been noted for his independence from Dress Regulations.'

With all that said, let us now set about enjoying a sample of what talented people have placed on paper and canvas for centuries. In this, the fourth in my 'Guide to Military Art' series, I have divided the book into two sections. The first will show images of military bands and those that played in them—drummers, trumpeters, buglers, pipers and players of brass instruments of all shapes and sizes, marching or standing still. Section Two then moves on to what I believe will become a popular collecting theme of the future—the military sheet music cover. Featuring uniformed soldiers, these colourful items can often prove to be as valuable as an historic record of dress as any published print. And just as delightful to own, too.

# SECTION ONE – BANDS AND BANDSMEN

## 1 – RULE BRITANNIA

Pencil and wash drawing by Richard Mounteney Jephson. As two ships in the distance battle against a cruel sea, a small boat struggles to get to the safety of dry land. Its crew, one of them turbaned, seem Indian. Standing, and seemingly unnerved by the situation, a band with assorted brass instruments, and even a bassoon, plays on with the tune of 'Rule Britannia'. Steady on their feet, three officers stand aft with the Colours while the drum major, who can be seen singing, leads from the front just as he would have done when taking part in some parade or other. The bass drummer is in good voice too as, standing next to his bandmaster, he beats time. *(Image courtesy of the Anne SK Brown Military Collection, Brown University Library)*

## 2 – THE BALLARD SINGERS

Hand-coloured and undated aquatint entitled 'The Ballard Singers'. A veteran Scottish soldier wearing a blue diced cap, a red coat with blue collar, blue shoulder straps with white worcestered tufts and blue lace around the buttonholes sings loudly as he accompanies himself on a violin. His battle-hardened uniform is torn and heavily patched and what is left of his right leg terminates into a long wooden peg. He has his family with him. A young boy, barefoot and wearing a long ill-fitting blue coat which at night-time possibly serves as a blanket, holds an empty cap out for some reward. His mother, holding her torn husband steady by hanging onto the tails of his regimental coat, sings out too. She is also dressed shabbily, her brown, patched cloak doing much to keep warm a smiling baby who, for now, just listens to the pleading music.

The veteran soldier and his stout wife sing on and await the appearance of somebody, coins in hand, hopefully, at the grey door. Behind them, a street of tall buildings, a church spire and a bell tower which is, for now, silent. *(Image courtesy of the Anne SK Brown Military Collection, Brown University Library)*

## 3 – BANDSMAN, 92ND (GORDON HIGHLANDERS) REGIMENT OF FOOT

An original unsigned and undated watercolour painting featuring a bandsman of the 92nd (Gordon Highlanders) Regiment of Foot around 1815. He wears a short white jacket with high yellow collar, yellow cuffs, red piping across the chest, on the collar and sleeves and yellow shoulder straps terminating in red wings. The gold buttons carry the numeral 92. Worn over the kilt, a white hair sporran with gold top, five yellow and red tassels and a triangular gold badge displaying the figure of a Sphinx over the numeral 92. The headdress is a black feather bonnet with diced border and red over white plume. The hose are tied with red ribbon, the black shoes having oblong gold buckles. A black shoulder belt is worn to which is fixed an oblong gold plate engraved with the Cross of St Andrew, a sphinx and the Roman numerals XCII. A French horn is carried in the right hand, the left holding a length of looped gold cord. Six other bandsman dressed the same, two holding trumpets, form a line against a high wall in the distance. One, wearing a white apron over his uniform, stands beside a large drum. To the right of the drum, drummers in red coats stand holding drumsticks, the white leather slings used to hold their instruments clearly visible in this detailed image. Out in front of them, and wearing a crimson sash over the left shoulder, stands the drum major. *(Image courtesy of the Anne SK Brown Military Collection, Brown University Library)*

## 4 – 17TH LIGHT DRAGOONS (LANCERS), REVIEW ORDER

In this print from William Spooner of 377 Strand, London, little detail can be seen of the passing lancers as they approach in review order from the right. But the artist's sideways study of the mounted band, however, does offer much in its perspective. See, for instance, how the cap lines fall quite distant from the headdress before they pass under the right arm, and how the saddlecloth is kept in place by passing the horse's tail through a leather loop. The image is from Spooner's 'The British Army' series of fifty-three plates, drawn by MA Hayes, engraved by J Lynch and printed by W Kohler of 22 Denmark Street, London.

## 5 – KETTLEDRUMMER, 10TH (PRINCE OF WALES'S OWN) HUSSARS

From *Bands of the British Army* by WJ Gordon, published by Frederick Warne & Co, Ltd with illustrations provided by Frederick Stansell. No publication date is given by Warne, but a prefatory note from them in the book tells how 'The main feature of the pictures in this book (which are from water-colour drawings made by Mr. Stansell just before the war) is the complete series of the drummers of the cavalry regiments with their drum-banners and drum-horses.' This is indeed a feature of the book, the c1914 cavalry regiments all being represented among the sixty-eight individual musicians in the work.

Frederick Stansell had based this painting on the 10th Hussars drum horse he had seen at Hyde Park on the occasion of the King's coronation day, 9 August 1902. The blue banners display the Prince of Wales's plumes within a crowned strap embroidered with the regimental title in gold lettering. Three battle honours appear on blue scrolls either side, that for South Africa being place separately below. In 1903 the 10th Hussars left for a tour of duty in India, leaving behind at the same time the grey horse shown in the illustration.

## 6 – ROYAL WELCH FUSILIERS, 1742

Dated 1742, the first colour image of uniform in Major Rowland Broughton-Mainwaring's, *Historical Record of the Royal Welch Fusiliers* shows a party of eleven fusiliers and drummers at rest. On a grassy mound a cooking pot has been set up, weapons have been piled while a figure holding a tall pike looks on with interest as a drummer adjusts his snares. During the summer of 1741, the 23rd Royal Welsh Fusiliers were encamped on Lexden Heath close to Colchester, Essex. But there would soon be trouble brewing in Europe and with this in mind King George II ordered an army of 16,000 men under Field-Marshall the Earl of Stair to make ready for war in the Netherlands. On 28 April 1742 the 23rd was reviewed on Kew Green by the king and in the following month embarked for Flanders. Published in 1889 by Hatchards, there is no reference made in Major Broughton-Mainwaring's book as to artist; the printer Vincent Brooks Day & Sons Ltd is, however, credited with the production of each image.

## 7 – 2ND DRAGOON GUARDS (QUEEN'S BAYS)

Headed by the regimental band, the 2nd Dragoon Guards (Queen's Bays) turn a sharp corner into a dusty lane. The column is led by the regiment's drum horse, the kettledrummer being shown as a corporal who wears white aiguillettes from the left shoulder. The drum banner is buff, following the facing colour of the Bays, and has below a gold embroidered wreath the single battle honour Lucknow. Note how the helmet plumes of the band are white in marked contrast to the black of the regimental plumes. From *Our Armies* by Richard Simkin.

## 8 – MUSIK BANDA DER KK DEUTSCH. LIN. INFANT

There is a commotion going on in this picture by Franz von Hauslab. Dressed in blue, their coats decorated with gold, two cavalrymen with swords drawn can be seen in the left foreground, seemingly in the act of controlling the gathered crowd. None, except possibly the top-hatted man on the right who is about to run off, seem at all bothered. Excited dogs bark, the owners of one of them out for the afternoon with their young son. They have come to see the troops. With rolling hills and a city skyline in the distance, in from the left come an infantry battalion led by an officer who must at any time soon pull up his men so as to let the band pass. With this in mind, nervously the drum major looks to his left. This lithograph was published by Joseph Trentsensky in 1823. *(Image courtesy of the Ann SK Brown Military Collection, Brown University Library)*

## 9 – 1st IRISH REGIMENT OF HORSE, 1751

In 1746 several of the British Army's regiments of horse were re-styled as dragoon guards and with this change the 5th Horse assumed the new title of 1st Irish Horse. Moving on now to 1751 and a warrant issued that year on 1 July regarding cavalry uniform, it was now directed that the 1st Irish Horse should adopt hats ornamented with silver lace and a black cockade, scarlet coats faced with pale blue, the buttonholes to be worked in white with white metal buttons. Waistcoats and breeches were to be pale blue, the red cloaks to be

lined with the same colour. The warrant also dealt with horse furniture which was to be pale blue with a border of broad white mohair lace with a scarlet stripe down the centre, and the numeral 1 over the letter H embroidered on a red ground within a wreath of roses and thistles. The new changes are reflected accurately in this signed Richard Simkin watercolour. A kettledrummer appears to the left of the image, his blue coat being faced red and heavily adorned with white lace with a red stripe. Traditionally the colours of drummers' coats at this time were the reverse of those worn by the regiment, in this case light blue with red facings instead of red with light blue. Unseen in the picture are the drummer's red waistcoat and breeches. *(Image courtesy of the Ann SK Brown Military Collection, Brown University Library)*

## 10 – DRUMMER, 9th (THE EAST NORFOLK) REGIMENT OF FOOT

An original watercolour painting by Richard Caton Woodville. The drummer wears a white coat with white breeches, black gaiters and an 1812-1816-pattern black shako with brass plate bearing the number 9. Plaited white cord runs below the brass plate which terminates in tassels up on the right side. White lace, which has a central blue wavy stripe, decorates the front of the jacket, the inner seam of the sleeves, the arms, shoulder wings and cuffs. A red lining can just be seen on the turnback by the right hand, the same red cloth being just visible on the inner side of the shoulder wing. A buff belt holding the brass-tipped scabbard seen hanging down at the back has an oblong brass plate stamped with the figure of Britannia, the regiment's ancient badge. Plaited white cord hangs from the rope tension drum which is hooked to a wide buff belt worn over the left shoulder—the two brown leather tubes being to hold the drumsticks when not in use. The regimental facing colour, yellow, is seen on the face of the drum. The hoops, top and bottom, are red with a blue wavy line on white. *(Image courtesy of the Ann SK Brown Military Collection, Brown University Library)*

## 11 – COME AND JOIN US BROTHERS

The United States War Department established the Bureau of Coloured Troops via General Order on 22 May 1863. It was the time of the Civil War and in the North recently freed slaves were invited to join the Union Forces as members of cavalry, infantry and artillery regiments. Some 178,000 would enlist into what became known as the United States Coloured Troops thanks to a strong recruiting programme. In the poster illustrated, eighteen African-American infantrymen stand wearing grey greatcoats, trousers and capes and blue caps with bugle-horn badges on the crown. Posing in front of a Sibley tent

and the American flag, they each have leather shoulder belts with oval brass plates and waistbelts fitted with an ammunition pouch and socket bayonet. The young drummer boy has a grey jacket and trousers, both decorated with red, and a red cap.

In February 2017 the US auctioneers Cowan's offered for sale a copy of the poster illustrated. Describing it as a chromolithograph by PS Duval & Son of Philadelphia, Cowan's in their catalogue description refers to a 'Photo Sleuth' feature in the Autumn 2015 issue of *Military Images* which gives much information as to the origins of the picture and its possible subjects. Originally a photograph taken indoors, the article suggests that the men are from the 25th USCT, the location being Camp William Penn in Philadelphia. The white officer, possibly George Edwin Heath, the post, adjutant of the camp and a lieutenant in the 6th USCT.

I have managed to trace a copy of the photograph used for the poster on the 'Black Military History' website. Against a plain studio background, the eighteen troops and their officer are the same, but there is no drummer boy. The regiment is identified as the 25th which, notes the item, sailed for the Gulf of Mexico soon after the photograph was taken where it formed part of the garrison of New Orleans and later Pensacola.

'Once let the black man get upon his person the brass letters U.S.,' wrote abolitionist Frederick Douglass, 'let him get an eagle on his button, and a musket on his shoulder, and bullets in his pocket, and there is no power on the earth or under the earth which can deny that he has earned the right of citizenship in the United States.'

## 12 – BEATING UP FOR RECRUITS

In this hand-coloured engraving published on 1 November 1781 by Robert Sayer and John Bennett of 53 Fleet Street, London, an officer of the Coldstream Guards temptingly dangles a purse of money before four potential recruits. To assist him in his task, a drummer beats out encouragement on a drum emblazoned with the regimental badge. Artist John Bennett has set the scene outside a village inn with a horse-drawn waggon passing in the distance. *(Image courtesy of the Ann SK Brown Military Collection, Brown University Library)*

## 13 – DI BRAVE TAMBOUR

Lithographic plate by and after August von Pettenkofen showing an Austrian drummer during the heat of battle running from a burning building carrying a child. Publisher, LT Neumann. *(Image courtesy of the Ann SK Brown Military Collection, Brown University Library)*

## 14 – A RECRUITING PARTY

Hand-coloured etching caricature by Isaac Cruikshank after George Moutard Woodward and published by Allen & West of 15 Paternoster Row, City of London on 18 February 1797. Assisted by a young drummer and fifer, and officer attempts to persuade two civilians that life in King George's army is for them. One looks horrified at the thought of it, while the other seems quite excited at the idea. *(Image courtesy of the Ann SK Brown Military Collection, Brown University Library)*

## 15 – THE AUKWARD SQUAD OR ENRAGED SERGEANT

Dressed in their reds, greens and blues, a party of volunteer recruits stumble and fumble over their drill as a red-faced sergeant, waving his cane high, screams his orders without success. Looking on, a young fifer and drummer are enjoying the spectacle, having, no doubt, seen it all before. A hand-coloured aquatint caricature after Thomas Rowlandson published on 17 July 1798 by Rudolph Ackermann of 101 Strand, London. *(Image courtesy of the Ann SK Brown Military Collection, Brown University Library)*

## 16 – WINGING A SHY COCK

A hand-coloured etched satire in reference to General John Whitelocke who, having been appointed commander of an expedition to Buenos Aires in 1807, went on to lead his troops in a disastrous and costly campaign. After sustaining heavy losses, surrender negotiations were undertaken resulting in the British abandoning Montevideo and returning home. Whitelocke's conduct was seen as cowardly by not only the army, but the general British public too. He was brought before a court martial held at the Royal Hospital, Chelsea in 1808 which

would find him guilty on all but one of the several charges brought against him. Dismissed from the army, John Whitelocke retired to Beaconsfield in Buckinghamshire where he died on 23 October 1833.

Artist Isaac Cruikshank shows the general in utter disgrace having his sword broken and epaulettes and buttons ceremoniously removed by two drummer boys. To the right, a fife lays upon the open music to 'The Rouge's March'. Mockingly, the devil offers a way out of his shame via a pistol, but the petrified general can only ask if the flint has been taken out. 'Winging a Shy Cock' was published by Samuel William Fores of 50 Piccadilly, London on 29 March 1808. *(Image courtesy of the Ann SK Brown Military Collection, Brown University Library)*

## 17 – THE 7TH HUSSARS ENTERING LONDON FOR ROAD DUTY ON THE OCCASION OF A ROYAL VISIT

This postcard features the 7th Hussars led by its mounted band on the occasion of its entering London for road duty during a Royal Visit. Mr RG Harris, in his detailed study of mounted bands written for the Military Historical Society, tells how on its return to England from South Africa in 1905, the Regiment was stationed at Norwich until October 1907 when it moved to Aldershot. A new drum-horse named 'Tom' had been obtained by this time and this is the animal shown in Harry Payne's artwork. Keeping it in the family, the detailed architectural background has been provided by Harry Payne's brother, Arthur. Publisher, Raphael Tuck & Sons.

## 18 – BAND OF THE 12TH (EAST SUFFOLK) REGIMENT, 1861-1871

Colour plate facing page 298 of *History of the 12th (The Suffolk) Regiment 1685-1913* by Lieutenant-Colonel EAH Webb, published by Spottiswoode & Co, Ltd, London in 1914. The musicians wear white

tunics with yellow facings and red piping, their shakos being of the 'Albert' pattern with peaks front and back and white over red pom-poms. For the drum major, a scarlet tunic.

## 19 – 17TH LIGHT DRAGOONS ON SERVICE IN AMERICA, 1775

The last section in *Our Armies,* written and illustrated by Richard Simkin, is headed 'The British Army of the Past' and includes six full-page plates and sixteen smaller colour illustrations. The 17th Light Dragoons are shown here in the year 1775, the trumpeter wearing the reverse of the regimental colours, viz, white with scarlet facings, as opposed to the scarlet with white seen being worn by the officer on the right. Simkin notes that his illustration depicts the 17th as it appeared at the time of the American War of Independence. The regiment was, in fact, the first cavalry corps to cross the Atlantic, being present at Bunker's Hill and most of the subsequent campaigns from 1776 to 1781 when it returned to Ireland. The regiment was re-designated as 17th (Duke

of Cambridge's Own) Lancers in 1876.

## 20 – DRUM MAJOR OF THE ROYAL ARTILLERY, C.1840

Frontispiece to *The History of the Dress of the Royal Regiment of Artillery 1625-1897* compiled and illustrated by Captain RJ Macdonald, RA and published in 1899 by Henry Southern & Co of 140 Strand and 37 Piccadilly, London.

## 21 – DRUM MAJOR AND DRUMMER OF THE 33RD REGIMENT OF FOOT, DUKE OF WELLINGTON'S FUNERAL, 1852

Colour plate after PW Reynolds dated 1852 opposite page 264 of *History of the Thirty-Third Foot* by Albert Lee, published by Jarrold & Sons, Ltd, The Empire Press, Norwich in 1922. The 33rd Regiment had been brought from Manchester to attend the funeral of the Duke of Wellington, Albert Lee noting that, 'It was

a day of mingled distress and pride for the regiment, which paraded at 5 o'clock on the morning of the 18th of November and marched in rear of the Horse Guard's parade, where it took up position with the other regiments composing the funeral escort.' The duke, as Arthur Wellesley, had served for thirteen years as lieutenant-colonel of the 33rd and, at the death of Lord Cornwallis in June 1806, became its colonel. 'During the lifetime of Wellington', records Lee, 'it had often been suggested in military quarters that the Duke's name should be intimately and very definitely connected with that of the 33rd', but at Wellington's request, this honour was postponed until his death. It then followed that on 18 June 1853 the officer commanding the 33rd Regiment received the following notification from Horse Guards: 'Her Majesty has been graciously pleased to command that the 33rd Regiment of Foot shall henceforward bear the name of The 33rd (or The Duke of Wellington's) Regiment.' This honour was to give the corps, 'the peculiar distinction' (Albert Lee again) 'of being the only British regiment named after a subject—not Royal.' Black cloth for military funerals is much in evidence in Reynolds's image.

## 22 – HIS LIBERTY IS FULL OF THREATS TO ALL

Published c.1880 by George Routledge & Sons was a book containing twenty-four colour lithographs linked with one-line quotes from the works of William Shakespeare. This was the *Military Misreadings of Shakspere,* the spelling of the Bard's name being that of its author who appears on the title page as 'Major Seccombe.' The plates take the form of cartoons, each measuring eight by six-and-half inches, their captions occupying the whole page opposite. Throughout the book, a number of images represent no particular formation, just groups of uniformed characters, but many can indeed be associated with certain regiments thanks to the artist's attention to detail. Could members of those regiments possibly be offended? Well, Major Seccombe must certainly have been aware of this, as after the contents pages of his book he adds, 'In submitting these Military Caricatures to the public, the artist would disclaim all intention of reflecting upon the powers of equitation, etc., of any particular corps, the uniforms of the regiments represented having been chosen solely for variety.' Major Seccombe was in fact Major Thomas Strong Seccombe (1840-1913), a British Royal Artillery Officer.

In Shakespeare, of course, it was Hamlet himself whose liberty posed the threat. But on this occasion it is a loose horse belonging to either the Berkshire or Buckinghamshire Yeomanry Cavalry (see letters behind saddle) that caused the problem. As brass instruments and their owners go crashing to the ground, and the drum major thinks that he has never seen the like in all of his thirty five years' service, the part-time military horse seems quite happy among the regulars—and an elite Grenadier Guards band at that. Quotation, *Hamlet,* Act iv, scene 1.

## 23 – KING'S OWN SCOTTISH BORDERERS

Here we have the not-too-often seen bassoon. Held on the right-hand-side of the instrument by a brass spring clip in the shape of a lyre, the sheet music sits at a position enabling the bandsmen to see his copy whilst on the march. The musician wears a scarlet doublet with dark blue facings and tartan trews. Helmets were worn by the regiment until July 1903 when the more Scottish-in-appearance headdress, the Kilmarnock bonnet, was taken into use. Image from *Bands of the British Army* by WJ Gordon, published by Frederick Warne & Co, Ltd with illustrations after Frederick Stansell.

## 24 – SUFFOLK REGIMENT

As can be seen in Frederick Stansell's painting of a Suffolk Regiment bandsman, the lyre sheet music holder is positioned upright on the clarinet,  as opposed to side mounted as in the previous image. The artist shows the yellow facings restored to the regiment in place of white in 1899 and has given the musician both the Queen's and King's Medals awarded for service during the Second Boer War in South Africa, 1899-1902. From *Bands of the British Army* by WJ Gordon, published by Frederick Warne & Co, Ltd.

## 25 – CONNAUGHT RANGERS

WJ Gordon, in *Bands of the British Army*, refers to the brass instrument encircling the bandsman as a 'bombardon'. Perhaps better known outside military music as the tuba, the bombardon was the first brass instrument to be fitted with valves and is placed (worn, even) encircling the body when marching. Another upright version resting on the lap is used in bands when seated. Artwork by Frederick Stansell.

## 26 – REMINISCENCES OF THE CAMP

Around about 1853, artist Henry Alken took himself down to Chobham in Surrey where he set about sketching camp life. With plenty to interest  him, Alken managed to gather enough material to put together six images. Pleased with his efforts, he then took the pictures to 31 Burlington Arcade. Piccadilly, London and the offices of Messrs Preston where happily, after litho work by Vincent Brooks, they were pleased to published them. And here is one of them. It features several officers of the 6th Dragoon Guards close to a tent: two of them chatting, another reading a newspaper as a fourth, inside, shaves. A brown dog sits contentedly in the foreground, whilst another (black this time) lends an ear to a band.

## 27 – PEACE PROCLAIMED

Twenty June 1814 and all is quiet in Europe. The treaty of Paris had been signed less than three weeks earlier, Napoleon had abdicated and got sent off to Elba, and peace was being enjoyed in Britain. At Edward Jarman's Royal Exchange in London, great crowds had turned out to hear the Heralds shout the good news in company with members of the Horse Guards, City Marshals, the Lord Mayor and a military band that included a black, mounted, drummer. Hand coloured engraving published on 28 June 1814 by George Thompson of 43 Long Lane, Smithfield in the City of London. *(Image courtesy of the Anne SK Brown Military Collection, Brown University Library)*

## 28 – 3RD REGIMENT OF FOOT

Here we have an unsigned and quite detailed colour plate of a black percussionist. Published around 1820 by J Wisehart, clearly the caption places the regiment as the 3rd of Foot, later in 1881 to take on the name of the Buffs, East Kent Regiment. But 'Gds' (Guards presumably) has been added in pencilled square brackets. *(Image courtesy of the Anne SK Brown Military Collection, Brown University Library)*

## 29 – DRUM HORSE, 3RD PRINCE OF WALES'S DRAGOON GUARDS

RG Harris, writing in 1963 (*Bulletin of the Military Historical Society,* Vol XIII) tells how, according to a note by F Stansell, the old blue drum banners of the 3rd Dragoon Guards were stolen by natives whilst serving in India sometime during its 1857 to 1867 and 1884 to 1892 tours. Frederick Stansell of course, responsible for the artwork in WJ Gordon's book, *Bands of the British Army.* Here we have one of the illustrations from that book. The kettledrummer sits on a piebald horse which has a black and red throat plume matching the musician's helmet plume. The yellow velvet drum banners in Stansell's painting, suggests RG Harris, were probably obtained for the 1897 Diamond Jubilee celebrations and feature the Prince of Wales's plumes with below, the battle honour Abyssinia.

## 30 – THE BRITISH AUXILIARY LEGION

The British Auxiliary Legion comprised ten battalions of infantry, a rifle corps, two regiments of lancers and supporting arms—a 'complete miniature army' as Conrad Cairns pointed out in a 1998 article published by the Society for Army Historical Research. Formed for service in Spain (1835-37), the legion was recruited in Britain from British subjects, '…but officially part of the Spanish forces, and paid by the Queen' (Conrad Cairns again). The legion was to take part in the First Carlist War and after a number of hard-fought battles and engagements returned to England for disbandment in December 1837. The print illustrated was produced by J Graf from litho work prepared by John West Giles.

The scene is somewhere in Spain and shows a mixed group of men from the legion led by a drummer wearing a red coat with yellow collar, shoulder straps, cuffs and turnbacks. He beats a rope tension drum, with apparently no embellishments, and displays the numeral 8 on his collar. Behind the drummer, carrying an axe and wearing a leather apron is a pioneer and further down the column several men seem to have grenade devices on the water canteens. A number are shown barefoot, their trousers torn at the knees and in tatters at the bottom. The last two figures, one of which is a woman who seems to be feeding a child, suggests a possible move to different quarters. Could the woman be wearing the greatcoat, with its numeral 3 on the collar, of the man in front? Her husband, possibly, who carries a number of cherished kitchen items from a former billet. *(Image courtesy of the Anne SK Brown Military Collection, Brown University Library)*

## 31 – DRUMMER, 5TH REGIMENT OF FOOT

This fine original watercolour signed and dated by Richard Simkin in 1881, shows a drummer of the 5th (Northumberland) Regiment of Foot wearing the tall-fronted shako (the 'Waterloo' Shako) in use from 1812 until replaced by the so-called 'Regency' pattern in 1816. The artist has not attempted to show in any great detail the crowned brass plate being worn, but an example showing that the numeral 5 was placed below the GR cypher can be seen on page 12 of *Head-dress Badges of the British Army,* Volume I by Arthur L Kipling and Hugh L King. A white buff-leather shoulder-belt is being worn with an oval plate. Once again Richard Simkin offers little or no detail, but the item may have followed the pattern then being worn at the time by officers of the regiment which had the regimental motto *Quo fata vocant* above the figure of St George and the dragon (see page 87 of *Military Shoulder-Belt Plates and Buttons* by Major HG Parkyn). The rope tension drum, with its red hoops, has regimental devices and the name of the regiment on a green ground at the front. *(Image courtesy of the Anne SK Brown Military Collection, Brown University Library)*

## 32 – THE 21st (ROYAL NORTH BRITISH FUSILIERS) REGIMENT OF FOOT, 1827

How small, even with his tall fusilier cap, the young drummer looks up against the colour sergeant on his right, and the officer on his left. Boys had been used as drummers in armies since medieval times and were used as young as twelve years old by the British, certainly during, if not before, the American War of Independence and at the Battle of Waterloo where one record mentions some 400 being employed.

The colour plate illustrated comes from *Historical Record and Regimental Memoir of The Royal Scots Fusiliers* by James Clark, a publication produced by Banks & Co of 12 George Street, Edinburgh at their Grange printing works in 1885. The book contains six colour plates (one of Colours, five of uniform) and no artist is mentioned.

The artist has set the scene within the walls and tall iron railings of a barracks, Windsor possibly where the regiment had moved for royal duties during the early months of 1827 and stayed until the Spring of the following year. Grenade badges are on the caps and on the oblong shoulder-belt plates. Tall white plumes are worn by all three solders, their scarlet coats having blue facings.

The lad holds a long brass bugle of the type that had a curl in the tubing just after the mouthpiece. His rope tension drum having been detached from a belt worn over both shoulders and placed on the floor, clearly seen now is the leather protector worn on the right thigh to save wear and tear on the trousers. Drumsticks are being held securely on the yellow section of the belt. Note how the artist has included the Roman numerals 'XXI' within the colour sergeant's rank insignia.

## 33 – THE ROYAL SCOTS FUSILIERS, PIPER AND BANDSMAN 1894

The 21st (Royal North British Fusiliers) Regiment of Foot had been re-designated as Royal Scots Fusiliers in 1881. We have learnt from the previous illustration how a history of the regiment by James Clark had been published in 1885. Ten years later a new version was to appear under the title of *History of the Royal Scots Fusiliers,* this time by Lieutenant-Colonel Percy Groves and published by W & AK Johnson of Edinburgh and London with eight colour plates of uniform after Harry Payne.

The last plate (Plate VIII) is illustrated here and features a piper and bandsman for the year 1894. The former, his pipes tucked safely under his arm, is wearing 42nd pattern tartan and a plain glengarry cap with black cock's feathers. The latter, his instrument this time resting at his side, wears a fusilier fur cap, scarlet doublet with blue facings and tartan trews. Unseen is the tall grenade badge bearing the royal arms that was worn at the front of the cap. Similar, but smaller, however, is the version clearly seen on the bandsman's white buff-leather pouch. Just a hint of the regiment's white embroidered grenade over RSF shoulder title is evident. Regarding tartan, it was not until 1928, in commemoration of the regiment having been raised by Charles Erskine, 5th Earl of Mar in 1678, that Erskine tartan was adopted.

## 34 – 26TH (CAMERONIANS) REGIMENT OF FOOT, 1812

Arthur Sharpin White's most valuable reference work, *A Bibliography of Regimental Histories of the British Army,* makes mention of a book to the regiment with the following publication information: edited by Thomas Carter, Adjutant-General's Office, Horse Guards, Byfield, Stanford & Co, 1867. Entitled *Historical Record of the Twenty-Sixth, or Cameronian Regiment,* the book contains two colour plates of uniform and one of colours. The former head of the War Office Library then goes on to say how a few copies were produced containing twenty-four colour plates of uniform after Richard Simkin. Turning now to the Army Museums Ogilby Trust's most excellent reference work, *Index to British Military Costume Prints 1500-1914,* we learn how the volume containing the additional twenty-four lithographs by Simkin was in fact a reprint of the first (with additional material) published c1883.

Here illustrated is plate No 6 from the second book which features a drummer and officer from the year 1812. Richard Simkin always good for detail, shows the drummer's fur cap with a brass plate bearing the cypher GR below a crown. As was the custom, reversed regimental colours are worn by the musician (see the accompanying figure of an officer who wears a scarlet coat with yellow facings), in this case yellow for the jacket and scarlet or red for the collar and cuffs. The same GR cypher appears on the officer's crowned shako plate.

## 35 – 26TH (CAMERONIANS) REGIMENT OF FOOT, 1854

The year 1854 almost immediately suggests the opening of the Crimean War. At the time, however, the 26th was located in both Canada and Bermuda where at the latter station the regiment suffered much loss due to an outbreak of yellow fever. Still with the c1883 history mentioned in the previous plate, Richard Simkin has treated us this time to a splendid trio of musicians in the form of the drum-major, a piper and trombonist. The latter's white cap, with its diced band, clearly shows the number 26. The kilted piper wears a Highland bonnet with tall red plume, that of the drum-major being draped over the headdress from the left side. The sash worn over the left shoulder is yellow and has a pair of token drumsticks held in position just below the regimental badge of a mullet star. Just visible under the sash, and on a white shoulder-belt, is an oblong plate which at the time would have displayed a crowned mullet within a wreath, a Sphinx superscribed Egypt and the dragon awarded for service during the China campaign.

## 36 – 26TH (CAMERONIANS) REGIMENT OF FOOT, 1868

Still with the c1883 history of the 26th (Cameronians) Regiment mentioned in the previous images, we move on to the year 1868 and a Simkin plate showing a bugler and bandsman. Scarlet coated, his shako topped with a white-over-red ball tuft, the bugler stands with his instrument resting on his right hip. A green cord is attached which has two tassels just below the left shoulder. Returning to the headdress, Richard Simkin has correctly given the soldier the shako, with its crowned star-shape badge showing the regimental number within a Garter, which was worn between 1855 and 1869.

The regiment easily identified by the number 26 in the white cap, the bandsman on the left of the image is shown in a white jacket edged with red. The yellow regimental facing colour appears on the collar, cuffs and shoulder wings. The 26th had taken part in the 1868 Expedition to Abyssinia and Simkin has recalled this by giving the bandsman the medal, with its white-red-white ribbon, awarded to those that took part in that campaign. Both men wear bandsman swords suspended from white buff-leather waistbelts, the clasps of which again show the regimental number.

## 37 – 26TH (CAMERONIANS) REGIMENT OF FOOT, 1879

Richard Simkin this time from the c1883 regimental history mentioned previously shows three members of the regiment wearing the home service helmet. Only introduced into the British Army just a year before the date given to the image, it bore a crowned star plate with the numeral 26 within a Garter strap. Two musicians are shown, a drum-major in the centre and a young drummer on the right. The regimental number appears again, this time just below the token drumsticks held on the drum-major's yellow sash. A shallow side drum is being played by the drummer, the tension of the instrument being adjusted not by rope, but metal rods which are seen here painted red. The same colour also for the worm lines around the top and bottom rims. A white leather uniform protector worn on the left leg down almost to the knee has been included by the artist. Lastly, and on the left, is a pioneer of the regiment who can be identified by the crossed axes worn on the upper right arm. Traditionally, pioneers were allowed to wear beards.

## 38 – THE CAMERONIANS REGIMENT OF FOOT, 1713

With numbers yet to form part of their titles, regiments in 1713 were known by the names of their colonel,

in this case, Lieutenant-General George Person who had been appointed on 24 August 1706. He served until replaced by Lieutenant-General Philip Anstruther, Member of Parliament for Anstruther Easter Burghs 1715 to 1741 and 1747 to 1754, in May 1720. But in 1713 the title The Cameronians was also in use by the future 26th Regiment of Foot.

Here in this original watercolour painting by Charles Lyall (one of 126 images by this artist held by the Anne SK Brown Military Collection) we see a piper wearing a red coat with wide yellow cuffs and lining. The waistcoat is yellow too and is edged with a line of white lace. The tricorn hat has a diced band and tall brown feather rising up from behind a silver badge or button. Tight-fitting tartan trews are being worn which are tied at the bottom with green ribbons, and the black shoes have silver buckles. *(Image courtesy of the Anne SK Brown Military Collection, Brown University Library)*

### 39 – SAPPERS AND MINERS, DRUMMER 1787

From artist Charles Lyall, an original signed watercolour which he entitles 'Sappers & Miners Drummer' with a date of 1787. Military engineers had existed since c1414, but the Soldiers Artificer Company formed to construct fortifications at Gibraltar in 1772 is considered to be the first permanent engineers of the British Army. Under the command of officers of the Royal Engineers, the Gibraltar Company was absorbed into the Royal Military Artificers in 1797, this title in 1812 being changed to Royal Sappers and Miners. In turn, this corps was absorbed into the Royal Engineers in 1856. The blue coat is decorated down the front and sleeves, around the collar and shoulder straps and on the coat tails with yellow lace dotted with red crowns. The artist illustrates clearly how the drum's tension rope works its way down from the top (drum head) hoop to the bottom while passing through white leather tugs. It then terminates in a chain link pattern drag rope hanging down below the bottom head upon which the snares are visible. *(Image courtesy of the Anne SK Brown Military Collection, Brown University Library)*

### 40 – BOMBAY SAPPERS AND MINERS, BUGLER 1903

Another original watercolour by Charles Lyall from the Anne SK Brown Military Collection, this time of a bugler from the Bombay Sappers and Miners. Dated 1903, the sideways-on figure is wearing a red jacket with blue collar and cuffs, blue trousers with a narrow red stripe, blue putties, brown boots and a brown leather waistbelt. Yellow lace forms the shoulder straps and an Austrian knot at the cuff. This corps had originated in 1777 as a company of Pioneer Lascars and after several changes in title and organisation, became the Bombay Sappers and Miners in 1840. *(Image courtesy of the Anne SK Brown Military Collection, Brown University Library)*

### 41 – AN OFFICER'S FUNERAL, 5TH FUSILIERS 1870

Signed and dated 1870 by Harry Payne, this original watercolour sets a sombre scene. Just turning into a bend in the road, three of the leading party have been shown wearing the white with red stripes ribbon of the Indian Mutiny Medal. With their rifles caried slings upwards and tucked under the left arm, the fusiliers look down towards the ground as they negotiate the track. Behind them come the band dressed in white jackets with green facings and red braid around the collars and down the front. The regiment's grenade badges, bearing the figure of St George and the dragon, are clearly shown in the fur caps, as are hackles of red-over-green. Pulling the Union flag-draped coffin, which has the deceased officer's fur cap positioned on top, are five men from the Royal Field Artillery with busby caps fitted with white plumes and red busby bags. Then, led by officers wearing gold and crimson sashes, comes the battalion winding its way down from a distant hillside. *(Image courtesy of the Anne SK Brown Military Collection, Brown University Library)*

## 42 – TROMEPETER VOM KGL BAYERISCHEN NATIONAL-CHEVAULER REGIMENT, 1813

An original ink and watercolour drawing by Eduard Kohler who shows a Bavarian mounted trumpeter wearing a red coat with green collar, silver epaulettes and green trousers with red stripes. The broad-topped shako has silver cords and a wide, almost flag-like feather plume. Edged in white, the red saddlecloth bears the cypher of King Maximilian I Joseph of Bavaria. Eduard Kohler's date of 1813 brings to mind the previous year in which out of the 33,000 Bavarian troops that took part in the Russian Campaign, only some 4,000 returned.

*(Image courtesy of the Anne SK Brown Military Collection, Brown University Library)*

## 43 – BOCKPFEIFER DER ARTILLERIE

This unusual study in watercolours by Rudolph Trache shows a bockpfeifer (goat piper) of a Saxony artillery unit. He wears a long green coat lined with red and decorated across the chest with gold cord. Almost as long as his coat, a red waistcoat with more gold is worn with red breeches and yellow calf-length boots. The cap is red with a green bag and large gold ornament at the front. But what of his strange goat bagpipes? For an answer I turn to the website of the Bagpipe Society who tell how the instrument was, 'a large, low-sounding, fully single-reed bagpipe…' which had played an important part in the development of early German and Austrian folk music. *(Image courtesy of the Anne SK Brown Military Collection, Brown University Library)*

## 44 – TROMMLER UND HORNIST

The Anne SK Brown Military Collection place a date of 1735 on this hand-coloured copper engraving published in Vienna by Antla Gruber. The caricature shows two stout Austrian army musicians: on the left, a scarlet-coated kettledrummer and on the right, in blue this time, a trumpeter. *(Image courtesy of the Anne SK Brown Military Collection, Brown University Library)*

## 45 – PIPER OF A HIGHLAND REGIMENT, C.1825

A hand-coloured engraving of a single piper published by Le Petit in 1825. He wears a red coat with yellow collar and wide lapels, a rather shorter than usual tartan kilt and a sporran sporting at least eight tassels. The Highland bonnet has a diced band and tall white plume. An outdoor scene, the musician poses for the artist against a background of three tents and two other solders. *(Image courtesy of the Anne SK Brown Military Collection, Brown University Library)*

## 46 – AN OLD PERFORMER PLAYING ON A NEW INSTRUMENT

Here we have a piper of the 42nd Regiment in full Highland dress enjoying a new set of pipes in the form of the Emperor Napoleon—his legs for drones, arm for chanter and blue-coated body as the bag. A brilliant piece of satire from publisher SW Forbes who captions the image, 'An Old Performer playing on a New Instrument or one of the 42nd Touching the Invincible.' The print went on sale in September 1803 as a commemoration of the battle fought at Alexandria in 1801 in which the 42nd captured the Standard of Napoleon's so-called 'Invincible Legion.' *(Image courtesy of the Anne SK Brown Military Collection, Brown University Library)*

## 47 – BANDSMEN, 54TH (WEST NORFOLK) REGIMENT OF FOOT 1852

In this original watercolour painting by PW Reynolds we see both front and back views of two musicians from the 54th (West Norfolk) Regiment. On the right, the brass player stands with his instrument tucked under one arm. He wears an 'Albert' shako with red plume and cords, a white-tailed coat, which had a green ('popinjay green') collar, cuffs and turnbacks, and light blue trousers. Facing him in conversation, the bandsman is identified as such by the brass lyre badge at the front of his red cap. Clipped to an instrument, lyres acted as music holder when on the march. A short drill order jacket this time which has red shoulder cords and red lace on the collar, down the front on both sides and forming a point on the cuffs. *(Image courtesy of the Anne SK Brown Military Collection, Brown University Library)*

## 48 – DRUM MAJOR AND DRUMMER, 41st REGIMENT 1856

Here we have a colour plate after PW Reynolds from Lieutenant and Adjutant DAN Lomax's book, *A History of the Services of the 41st (the Welsh) Regiment (now 1st Battalion The Welsh Regiment) from its Formation in 1719 to 1895*. There were nine colour images (seven of uniform, two of colours) in total, the printers being Hiorns & Miller of Devonport in 1899. Clear on the cap of the drum major is the regimental number of 41. Both front and rear views of the uniform are provided by the artist, who has also showed the silver goat mascot at the head of the mace. Much red and gold lace for the drummer, the image showing how his leather uniform protector is secured to the left leg via two straps. His rope tension drum has a brass body and rims of a black-and-white 'Vandycked' pattern.

## 49 – TUBICEN AD MENSAM ELECTORALEM PELLIT CURAS RELEVATQUE DOLORES

The Anne SK Brown Military Collection date this hand-coloured copper-engraved plate by Pieter Schenck and captioned 'Tubicen ad Mensam Electoralem Pellit Curas Relevatque dolores', as 1680. It shows a young Duchy of Prussia musician wearing a blue coat decorated with gold lace playing a woodwind instrument (clarinet or oboe, possibly) before an attentive audience enjoying a meal—musicians perhaps, as one is seated on the upper head of a tenor drum. To the clarinet or oboe player viewing this picture, something would immediately jump out from the page as being wrong in the artist's positioning of the hands on the instrument. They should, just as can be seen in the group of players to the left, be arranged as left hand at the top, right hand at the bottom. Artistic licence possibly, but certainly right over left would make the instrument almost unplayable. A delightful and interesting image, nonetheless. *(Image courtesy of the Anne SK Brown Military Collection, Brown University Library)*

### 50 – A DRUMMER A DRUMMING A DRUM, 29TH (WORCESTERSHIRE) REGIMENT OF FOOT

An original watercolour signed by Filippo Severati (1819-1892) with the caption 'A Drummer a Drumming a Drum', showing a drummer boy wearing a tall fur cap with gold plate, white tassels and plume. His uniform is red with blue collar, cuffs and shoulder wings and the usual drummers' distinction of lace across the chest and down the arms. His rope-tension drum is emblazoned with the cypher of King George IV (therefore placing the period of the image as between 1820 to 1830) and the regimental number of 29. Note the two brown leather drumstick holders on the boy's white shoulder belt. Other drummers can be seen in the background, along with several fifers. But is the artist in error here, as the 29th Regiment had, since two years after its formation in 1694, worn facings of yellow? *(Image courtesy of the Anne SK Brown Military Collection, Brown University Library)*

### 51 – UNTERM SCHIRM – 'UNDER THE UMBRELLA'

From a sketch by Frankfurt artist Verlag von Hendschel, this postcard published by Martin Rommel & Co of Stuttgart shows a young German soldier saying farewell to his sweetheart sometime in 1914. On his back, his cello.

### 52 – A GERMAN TRENCH SCENE

As puffs of white smoke from shellfire dot the sky, safe for the time being in their deep and well-constructed trench, a group of German musketeers sing along to an accompaniment provided by an accordionist who encourages greater volume so as the girls back home can hear. A wartime postcard by a Berlin company with signature 'P.Hpy' at bottom left.

### 53 – PRINCE ALBERT'S (SOMERSETSHIRE LIGHT INFANTRY) (TERRITORIALS)

The scene is Annual Camp. In the background a covered wagon of the Army Service Corps accompanied by an infantryman in service dress and with rifle slopped, passes by on an already mud-drenched road. It had been a dry August, but a slight rain, horses, transport and battalions of marching feet have left their mark. Steady is the line of scarlet-clad Territorials, their sergeant having found them just enough dry ground to prevent the full-dressed detail from the slime. They are being inspected after all, the blue-frocked officer not so lucky with the mud. Awaiting orders, a young bugler stands by.

Somerset's response to the 1859 call for volunteer riflemen saw twenty-eight individually numbered corps raised by 1876. Higher organisations saw these merged as three, the Haldane reforms of 1907 demanding yet another consolidation, this time as his 4th and 5th Battalions, Prince Albert's (Somerset Light Infantry) (Territorial Force). Battalion headquarters: Bath (4th), Taunton (5th). Colour plate after Richard Caton Woodville from *His Majesty's Territorial Army* by Walter Richards (Virtue & Co, London 1910/11).

## 54 – STANSELL'S BANDSMEN

I was once advised by a respected publisher that, 'if you find a great picture, don't be afraid to use it time and time again.' Certainly, Frederick Stansell had similar thoughts as figures in four of the plates chosen for his *Soldiers of the King* publication will be recognisable as having been included in a future book—*Bands of the British Army* by WJ Gordon. Here in this full-page plate we have two drum horses and their riders, a drummer of the Coldstream Guards and a bugler from the Highland Light Infantry.

## 55 – THE TRUMPET CALLS

In this c1918 recruiting poster by Australian artist and writer Norman Lindsay, a brave bugler defies the enemy's fire. 'Come to the Front!' he seems to be calling to the distant civilian crowd—one has a ball under his arm, another a pick over the shoulder, in a bowler hat an office worker possibly, and a man with a whip—'Come and Help My Mates!' But reticent they look on from their daily and safe lives as 'The Trumpet Calls.' Norman Lindsay (1879-1969), no stranger to the propaganda brush and pen, certainly makes his point, the piercing eye and pleading hand of the musician saying it all.

## 56 – 79TH QUEEN'S OWN CAMERON HIGHLANDERS, 1893

In 1893 the Edinburgh and London firm of W & AK Johnston published *History of the 79th Queen's Own Cameron Highlanders*, a large format volume written by Lieutenant-Colonel Percy Groves. Although providing a useful potted history, the value of the book probably lies in its supporting full-page (ten inches by twelve) colour illustrations after Harry Payne.

Plate IV shows the regiment in 1893 against a backdrop of Edinburgh Castle. With bayonets fixed, the men are formed up in two ranks with an officer, sword drawn, standing to attention at the front. Mounted this time and wearing trews, another passes along the rows of kilted Highlanders and seems to be making some comment to one of the men. By his side, and doing his best to keep up, a bugler.

## 57 – ROYAL ENGINEER VOLUNTEERS

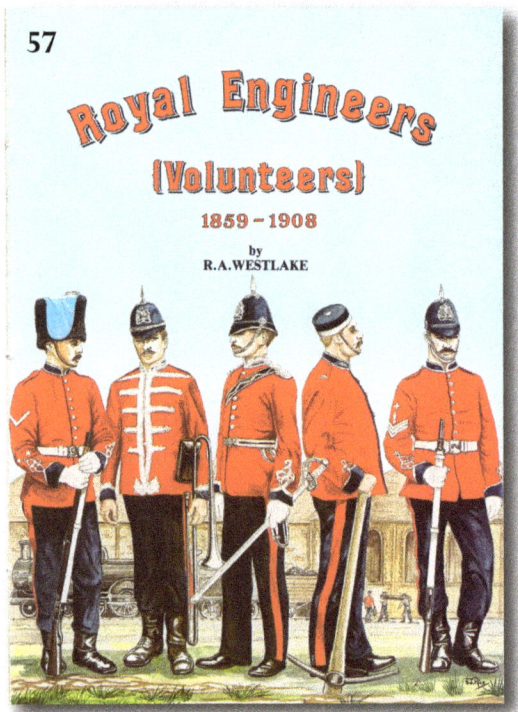

For my 1983 publication, *Royal Engineer (Volunteers) 1859-1908*, I asked the late George Rice to come up with a suitable cover illustration. A talented and obliging artist, George presented me with a group of five figures based on individual photographs from Colonel C Cooper-King's *The British Army and Auxiliary Forces*—published by Cassell and Co in 1893. Here we have volunteer sappers in a variety of headgear. There is an officer with sword, a bandsman with trombone, and with a pickaxe, one of the engineers from the Crewe railway town in Cheshire that wore a representation of a locomotive on their collars. Always providing great detail in his paintings, the artist shows some of the railwayman's colleagues hard at work in the background.

## 58 – THE BOLD HUSSARS

Published by Raphael Tuck & Sons, this image was produced as an item to be pasted into a scrapbook. Small pictures ('scraps'), especially printed for this purpose

were much in demand in Victorian times. The image shows a mounted hussar band passing through a wooded area led by two officers wearing blue jackets, crimson breeches and black busbies. The musicians are dressed the same, save for their white headdress. This uniform detail leads identification of the regiment to the 11th Hussars.

## 59 – THE DEATH OF MAJOR FRANCIS PEIRSON

The 95th Regiment was raised on 23 July 1779 in Yorkshire by Colonel John Reid, a well-known officer of the Black Watch. It took part in the January 1781 defence of Jersey in which one of the officers, Major Francis Peirson, was killed in the marketplace at St Helier. The regiment was disbanded in 1783.

Regarding Major Peirson's death, Tate Britain in London are in possession of an oil painting on canvas showing the event. By John Singleton Copley (1738-1815), the picture shows the young officer having just been shot by a French sniper being carried off by several men. Close by, and quick to react, is Major Peirson's black servant Pompey who can be seen shooting his master's slayer dead. To the left of the image a party of grenadiers move forward, a wounded drummer, supported by his instrument, seems to be waving farewell to his major. Terrified at the death and destruction all around, a mother with a young boy at her side and a baby in her arms runs from the scene to the right. The artist has accurately shown the troops wearing uniforms with buff facings, their breeches of the same colour. The Colour that flies high above the action has this too.

## 60 – THE WHITEHALL GUARD (2ND LIFE GUARDS) IN THE MALL

'The Whitehall Guard (2nd Life Guards) in the Mall' is Frederick Stansell's caption for this, his second colour plate in *Soldiers of the King*, published in London around 1902 by Frederick Warne & Co. With St James's Park on the left, we can assume that the detachment is on its way back to Knightsbridge Barracks having been relieved from duty at Horse Guards in Whitehall where the regiment had stood guard since the Restoration of King Charles II in 1660, a scene familiar to Londoners and tourists to this day. Scarlet are the jackets, blue the facings, the white-plumed steel helmets proudly displaying the Star of the Order of the Garter. As the 2nd Regiment of Life Guards, the blue cords running through the shoulder belts (the 1st have red) are correct. And all is well with the trumpeter who leads the column too, his red plume and white horse being correctly painted.

## 61 – GOODBYE AND GOOD LUCK

A carriage belonging to the London, Chatham & Dover Railway Company stands by as a drummer of the Grenadier Guards says farewell to his friend who is off to war. Artwork by Harold Hume Piffard (1867-1938), a London artist and one of the first British aviators. Publisher, Gale & Polden.

## 62 – THE DRUMMER'S COLOUR

A drum major and young drummer of the Northumberland Fusiliers are featured on this postcard after Edgar A Holloway. The artist sets the scene as St George's day, 23 April, upon which the regiment traditionally decorates the Colours, drums, drum major's staff and the men's headdress with roses. The tradition of a special colour carried by a drummer originates from 1762 and the Battle of Wilhelmstahl. At the head of a column of British troops, the old 5th Regiment of Foot charged forward into the French and in doing so managed to take, along with more than twice their number in prisoners, a French Standard. This much-cherished prize was then afterwards carried by a drummer. The original, however, would be lost in a fire at Gibraltar around 1834. Permission to produce a replacement was none too quick in coming and it would not be until Edward VII's time that the 'Drummer's Colour' was once again seen on a parade ground. Publisher, Gale & Polden.

## 63 – THE MARCH PAST

In Ernest Ibbetson's postcard artwork we see a battalion of the York and Lancaster Regiment marching past with Colours flying and bayonets fixed. The drummers stand by, the unusual rear view showing the white lace with its red crowns and how the curbed chin-chain of the helmet was hooked up below the spike having been unfastened from the right side. Publisher, Gale & Polden.

## 64 – THE FOUR O'CLOCK PARADE AT THE HORSE GUARDS

Whitehall, and crowds are gathered in the street to watch the parade. It's the turn of the 1st Life Guards today, artist Harry Payne showing them correctly in this postcard with red flask cords running through their white shoulder-belts. The trumpeter, with his red plume instead of white, is accurately drawn too. Seen at the end of the line, and sharing duty on this occasion, are two from the 21st Lancers. Publisher, Raphael Tuck & Sons.

## 65 – AN DIE GEWEHRE – GEPÄCK UMHÄNGEN!

'On with your weapons and your equipment' screams the order coming from the mounted figure on the right. Quickly the men lift heavy packs up onto their backs, adjust belts and gather up belongings. For the drummer, not to be left behind are his cloth-covered Pickelhaube helmet and, of course, his drum. From a postcard after Carl Becker (1820-1900).

## 66 – SUTLERESS AND DRUMMER, CATALONIAN REGIMENT

Paul Martin in his superb book *European Military Uniforms A Short History,* tells how the Romana Division was sent from Spain to form part of a Grand Army in 1807. Quickly a favourable impression was established by the troops, not only for their discipline but for their attractive regimental uniforms. Into Spain came the men accompanied by a very large baggage train, and even their wives and children. But pride in their uniforms was such that when on the march, plain civilian dress was worn so as to preserve their regimentals. The bass drummer seen here, seemingly unwilling to entrust his instrument to the baggage train, would no doubt be looking forward to a halt and an opportunity to enjoy the food and drink carried by his companion.

## 67 – BUGLER, 4TH ROXBURGHSHIRE RIFLE VOLUNTEER CORPS

Engraving from the *Illustrated London News.* The services of the 4th Roxburghshire Rifle Volunteer Corps at Hawick were accepted on 11 June 1860, the uniform being slate grey with red collars and black braid. Kilmarnock bonnets with a red pom-pom were worn, the belts, brown.

## 68 – BEFORE THE PARADE

Here we have a fine study by Bronislaw Gembarzewski of a kettle drummer and two trumpeters of the 1st (Polish) Lancer Regiment. From a copy of a *Le Sabretache Journal* of around 1895, the image shows the trumpeters' uniforms as white with red facings. The trousers, also red, are with red-and-white stripes down the legs. Worn on the headdress is a Maltese cross above a red-and-white cockade indicating a Polish unit in the service of France. On the drum banner is the emblem of the Chevau-Legers Polonais.

## 69 – QUEEN'S OWN ROYAL WEST KENT REGIMENT – THE DRUMS

The Drums of the Queen's Own Royal West Kent Regiment led by the drum major are shown marching past the guardroom in this original watercolour artwork produced by Ernest Ibbetson for one of Gale & Polden's postcard sets. Central is the bass drummer who wears a leopard-skin uniform protector, and behind him and the second rank are the fifers. *(Image courtesy of the Anne SK Brown Military Collection, Brown University Library)*

## 70 – THE SHERWOOD FORESTERS – FALL IN!

A busy parade ground scene as a young bugler sounds the 'Fall In'. The regiment's green facings are clear, as are the Maltese cross helmet plate centre and collar badge. As the original watercolour artwork supplied to postcard publishers Gale & Polden by Ernest Ibbetson, pencilled amendment notes can be seen in the right margin of the image. *(Image courtesy of the Anne SK Brown Military Collection, Brown University Library)*

## 71 – TRUMPETER, RUSSIAN LIFE GUARD CHASSEURS È CHEVAL

Hand-coloured lithograph after Alexandre Orlovski showing an outdoor study of a mounted Russian cavalry trumpeter. His instrument carried on his back, the musician wears a dark green uniform with red collar, lapels and cuffs. Much red and white (silver possibly) lace is worn on the deep shoulder wings and down the arms, and the trousers have a wide red stripe with a narrow central gold line. The same dark green cloth is used for the silver and red-edged saddle cloth, which carries the crowned cypher of Alexander I. *(Image courtesy of the Anne SK Brown Military Collection, Brown University Library)*

## 72 – HOUSEHOLD CAVALRY KETTLE DRUMMER AND TRUMPETER

An original watercolour painting signed by William Heath produced, according to the Anne SK Brown Military Collection, in 1840. Heath was born in 1794 and in fact died in Hampstead, London on 7 April 1840. The artist has gone to great lengths in his depiction of the ornate state uniforms of both musicians. Scarlet, gold, the royal arms in detail, even Queen Victoria's VR cypher is clear on both the chest of the drummer, and back of the trumpeter. A mounted officer of the Royal Horse Guards completes the image. *(Image courtesy of the Anne SK Brown Military Collection, Brown University Library)*

## 73 – A DRUMMER BOY ON BOARD SHIP

The Anne SK Brown Military Collection list the subject of this original watercolour painting as a Romanian drummer boy, the artist being Hermann Bittner, the work dated 1858. With discarded ropes all around, he poses before a stout mast, his uniform seemingly dirty and unkempt. The soft cap is blue with a red band, the jacket below the overcoat the same blue and with a red collar. Just above the drumstick holders on the shoulder-belt appears what seems to be a grenade device. *(Image courtesy of the Anne SK Brown Military Collection, Brown University Library)*

## 74 – PIPERS OF THE BLACK WATCH

With the city's castle looking down on the parade, and a gathered crowd enjoys the day, pipers of the Black Watch (Royal Highlanders) march proudly among the Edinburgh tramlines in this Conrad Leigh painting. Black Watch tartan for the drum major, Royal Stuart for the pipers.

## 75 – CORPORAL AND PIPER, CAMERON HIGHLANDERS

As two drummers chat in the background, a piper takes an opportunity to take the weight off his feet. A thick patent-leather belt rich in silver ornament crosses his green doublet, his cap badge, with its St Andrew's cross device, clearly seen on a plain glengarry. A thistle for the collar, the tartan is Cameron of Erracht. In this original watercolour artwork produced by Harry Payne, the corporal wears both the Queen's and King's Medals for South Africa. *(Image courtesy of the Anne SK Brown Military Collection, Brown University Library)*

## 76 – BANDSMEN, UNITED STATES ARMY 1888

The needs of any regimental band of the United States Army, it seems, could be supplied by GW Simmons & Co of Oak Hall, Boston, Massachusetts. Here in this magnificent chromolithograph by Julius Bien & Co we see a wide selection of the several uniforms available—fatigue, dress, something for the drum major, the Navy pattern and Newport Cadet Band—all numbered with descriptions printed below. 'In ordering' advises the supplier, 'be sure to give plate No. as well as No. of figure.' *(Image courtesy of the Anne SK Brown Military Collection, Brown University Library)*

## 77 – BRAZILIAN INFANTRY BANDSMAN, 1893

An original watercolour painting, signed and dated 1893 by Reginald Arthur, of a Brazilian musician wearing a green jacket with red facings and a wide black belt fastened by an oblong brass plate. Tucked into black boots, his trousers are light blue with a narrow red stripe. *(Image courtesy of the Anne SK Brown Military Collection, Brown University Library)*

### 78 – JOIN US IN AN IRISH REGIMENT

Two pipers (Royal Inniskilling Fusiliers left, Royal Irish Fusiliers right) feature in this recruiting poster.

### 79 – OFFICER AND TRUMPETER 6TH DRAGOON GUARDS, 1884

In this original watercolour painting by Orlando Norie we see an officer with drawn sword issuing an order to his trumpeter. Just visible in the musician's right hand is in fact a bugle, this smaller brass instrument, as opposed to the lager trumpet, used in cavalry regiments to send signals when mounted. Note the trumpeter's red plume distinction. *(Image courtesy of the Anne SK Brown Military Collection, Brown University Library)*

### 80 – TAMBOURS RUSSE ET ANGLAISE

The notes accompanying this watercolour from the Anne SK Brown Military Collection provide a date of 1818 and the suggestion that the image is possibly a copy of one of the engravings from the 'Collection de Costumes' series painted by Carle Vernet between 1818 and 1824. The blue-coated figure on the left is a drummer belonging to a Russian regiment, his drum perched high up above his head, his white greatcoat rolled across his chest, while that on the right is a rear view of another from Great Britain. Both wear swords and shakos with tall plumes. *(Image courtesy of the Anne SK Brown Military Collection, Brown University Library)*

### 81 – THE SPIRIT OF '76

For centuries drums have been used by the world's armies as a form of communication both on the parade ground and battlefield, and it would often fall to young boys to fill the role of drummers. The image of a child facing death on the battlefield seems to have appealed greatly to the artist and works featuring such commonplace scenes became popular among the art-buying public. Here we have a good example in the form of Archibald MacNeal Willard's painting *The Spirit of 76* or, as it was once known, *Yankee Doodle*. Possibly his most famous work, Willard shows three musicians at the head of their advancing regiment sometime during the American Revolutionary War. Clearly the brave, but frightened, boy on the left looks to the older man for guidance. A blood-stained bandage covers the blue-coated fifer's head; the white-haired veteran with his waistcoat open to the chest will undoubtably carry on come what may.

## 82 – STEADY THE FIFES AND DRUMS

In *Steady the Drums* by Lady Butler we move to the small Spanish village of Albuera where on 1 May 1811, a mixed British, Spanish and Portuguese force engaged the French in a fierce fight which saw casualties from both sides amount to some 7,000. Here in the painting we are looking at the drummers of the 57th (West Middlesex) Regiment of Foot which had a uniform of red coats with yellow facing. These are drummers, though, who traditionally have a reverse arrangement of, in this case, yellow jackets with red collars and cuffs.

Two bigger and possibly older boys, their fur caps still intact, stand confidently while a third, hatless and with his head bandaged, seems content to hold his position and accept whatever fate will be dealt to him. Younger boys are turning to the older for advice, a natural thing to do in the safety of the home depot when they were new to soldiering and their duty. In the face of death and destruction, they do it still. The drummers hold onto their drums, but one boy, killed or wounded, grips the leg of his friend. Behind the group, by a smashed cannon, a yellow-jacketed lad sits dazed and confused as, in the distance, his commanders direct what remains of their troops.

## 83 – ALLONS ENFANTS DE LA PATRIE – THE LAST PUSH

Encouraged by a drum major's cry of 'Let's go children of the Motherland', the sound of trumpets and the beating of drums, off the infantrymen go blindly towards the sound of battle. Grey and blue coated and with black kepis, with bayonets fixed, the men turn a decisive corner not knowing what lies ahead. Two men carry a ladder; another has been hit by a chance bullet and falls back. A 1920 painting by French illustrator 'Job' (Jacques Marie Gaston Onfroy de Bréville) (1858-1931).

## 84 – PIPING THE CAMERONS INTO A FRENCH VILLAGE

Colour plate from Sir James Edward Parrott's ten-volume set of books, *The Children's Story of the War,* showing pipers leading a battalion of the Cameron Highlanders across a stone bridge and into a French village. One man's kilt is quite visible, but note how the others protect theirs by canvas aprons. Artwork by D MacPherson, publisher Thomas Nelson & Sons.

## 85 – THE GLOUCESTERSHIRE REGIMENT

The rear view of the battalion formed up in the background, together with that of the gathered drummers, shows how the regiment's 'Back Badge' was worn on the helmets. A circular wreath with the figure of a Sphinx in the centre, the distinction had been awarded after the back-to-back action fought by the old 28th Regiment of Foot (later from 1881 the 1st Battalion Gloucestershire Regiment) during the 1801 campaign in Egypt. Note how for this Gale & Polden postcard, artist Ernest Ibbetson has included a lyre music holder protruding from the left side of the brass instrument held by the bandsman.

## 86 – TAPS, THE END OF THE DAY

Colour plate from Harper's *Pictorial Library of the World War*. Published in 1920, artwork by Sidney Riesenberg.

## 87 – DRUM MAJOR AND PIONEER OF A REGIMENT OF THE LINE

The regiment is unspecified in this plate after Charles Hamilton Smith and published in March 1815. Green would be the colour of its facings (see the bearded pioneer), the drum major and his two young drummers traditional wearing 'reversed' colours of green coats with red facings.

## 88 – KETTLEDRUMMER, MILITARY ORDER CUIRASSIER REGIMENT, 1805

In this detailed study of a Russian kettledrummer by military artist Bruce Bassett-Powell, we see a helmet of the 1803 pattern worn with a musicians' tall red crest. The badge is that of the Military Order of St George. A white jacket with black collar and cuffs is worn, its brass buttons being arranged in two rows surrounded by orange lace. The same material decorates the black shoulder wings, collar and both arms. The Military Order of St George appears on the black, gold-edged shabracque, and again together with the Imperial cypher at the front of the unusually shallow kettledrum. *(Image courtesy of Bruce Bassett-Powell)*

### 89 – MOROCCAN STATE TRUMPETERS

An original gouache painting signed and dated 1864 by Sir John Gilbert (1817-1897). Born in Blackheath, Surrey, Gilbert was knighted in 1872. *(Image courtesy of the Anne SK Brown Military Collection, Brown University Library)*

### 90 – AUSTRIAN MUSICIAN

Original watercolour by David Noël-Dieudonné (1797-1852) of an Austrian military musician playing an early version of a tuba. *(Image courtesy of the Anne SK Brown Military Collection, Brown University Library)*

### 91 – FRENCH MOBILE GARDE-INFANTRIE

Original ink and watercolour painting signed by E Bernard Derosne and featuring a drum major, drummer and several brass players. *(Image courtesy of the Anne SK Brown Military Collection, Brown University Library)*

### 92 – LE TROUBADOUR JOUANT DE SIX INSTRUMENTS

The Anne SK Brown Military Collection places this hand-coloured engraved plate as French c1815 at the time of the British occupation of Paris. Published by Pierre de La Mésangère, the image features a one-man band musician wearing a tall blue-over-yellow plume standing on a low stool while playing several instruments—pan pipes, a mandolin, a drum carried on his back which he beats with a drumstick tied to his left elbow and a triangle struck by a metal rod. Cymbals are affixed to the musician's calves and many small brass bells to his plume. Enjoying the entertainment, together with two young women, is a kilted Highland soldier on the right and, possibly, an Austrian infantryman on the left. *(Image courtesy of the Anne SK Brown Military Collection, Brown University Library)*

### 93 – A HIGHLAND PIPER C.1755

Original unsigned watercolour of a piper in Highland Dress posing in the open. He wears a short red jacket with light green collar, shoulder wings and cuffs and a diced black fur bonnet. His pipe bag and banner match the colour of his facings. *(Image courtesy of the Anne SK Brown Military Collection, Brown University Library)*

### 94 – AN INDIAN DEMON ATTACKING FORT DEFENDED BY EUROPEAN TROOPS

The Anne SK Brown Military Collection places this original unsigned native watercolour as around the time of the Mysore War of 1790 to 1792. Red-coated troops aim and fire their weapons as their six-toed attacker comes on, some of them having already been hit by arrows. Within a walled enclosure housing a number of cannons in towers, a woman stands on the balcony of a white building as musicians in yellow jackets trimmed red play encouragement to those defending their ground from this supernatural beast. *(Image courtesy of the Anne SK Brown Military Collection, Brown University Library)*

### 95 – DRUMMER OF THE 42ND REGIMENT

Colour plate after Edouard Detaille (1848-1912) engraved by Charles Gillot and published by Revue Illustrée in 1885. *(Image courtesy of the Anne SK Brown Military Collection, Brown University Library)*

### 96 – TAMBOUR BATTANT LA CHARGE

Original unsigned ink and watercolour painting by Auguste Raffet of a French drum major and two drummers on a mound during battle. *(Image courtesy of the Anne SK Brown Military Collection, Brown University Library)*

### 97 – CONFEDERATE CAVALRYMAN, 1861

Colour print of a mounted Confederate trumpeter wearing a yellow cap published by Gravure Française. *(Image courtesy of the Anne SK Brown Military Collection, Brown University Library)*

## 98 – 18TH (THE ROYAL IRISH) REGIMENT OF FOOT

Original watercolour signed and dated 1881 by Richard Simkin showing two standing figures, one a horn player, the other a black percussionist. The regiment's green facings provide the jacket colour of the latter, his large shoulder wings being fringed with green, white and red. Note how dark green cord has been bound around the tubing of the French horn.

## 99 – BAVARIAN MUSICIANS, 1806-1814

It's made of wood covered in leather and has finger holes rather than valves, but it's not a member of the woodwind family. Curved like a winding river seen from the air, its mouthpiece like that of a brass instrument, the serpent is, in fact, a distant relative of the tuba and is thought to have originated in France around 1590. And here in this highly detailed painting by military artist Bruce Bassett-Powell we see an example resting on the ground by its player. The detailed notes accompanying Bruce's image tell how, from 1800 to 1814, each Bavarian infantry regiment had its own band, numbers varying from between eight and sixteen in number. The figure on the left of our serpent player is the drum major of the 3rd (Prince Charles) Regiment; the clarinettist appearing on the right of the image is shown in standard Bavarian bandsman's uniform of the period. *(Image courtesy of Bruce Bassett-Powell)*

## 100 – BAVARIAN INFANTRY DRUMMER IN MARCHING ORDER, C.1832

Detailed drawing showing how the drum was carried on top of the pack when on the march. *(Image courtesy of the Anne SK Brown Military Collection, Brown University Library)*

## 101 – VIEW OF REGENT STREET

In this coloured lithograph by Thomas Picken after George Sidney Shepherd and published by Rudolph Ackermann, we see the Life Guards making their way down London's Regent Street towards Piccadilly Circus headed by state trumpeters and a kettledrummer. To the right, a crowd of men and women have interrupted

their shopping to watch the spectacle, some of them, no doubt, regular customers of Ackermann's print shop across the road at No 191. *(Image courtesy of the Anne SK Brown Military Collection, Brown University Library)*

## 102 – PIPER, 17TH (THE LOYAL) BENGAL INFANTRY 1901

An original watercolour by Charles Lyall showing a piper wearing a scarlet doublet with blue facings and white piping. The regimental badge of a large crescent moon can be seen in both the headdress and as an ornament on the wide black shoulder-belt. The Army List shows this regiment has having its headquarters at Agra. *(Image courtesy of the Anne SK Brown Military Collection, Brown University Library)*

## 103 – TAMBOUR DES ÉCOSSAIS

The artist, David Noël Dieudonné Finart, shows a rear view of a drummer in Highland dress wearing a yellow coat with red collar, shoulder wings, cuffs and turnbacks. He stands on high ground with a tented camp and mountains in the background. A French painter, Finart was born in 1797 and died in 1852. *(Image courtesy of the Anne SK Brown Military Collection, Brown University Library)*

## 104 – MUSICIEN DES ÉCOSSAIS

Another study by French artist David Noël Dieudonné Finart (see previous image) of a Highland musician. With arms folder, he wears a white jacket and holds a clarinet in his right hand. *(Image courtesy of the Anne SK Brown Military Collection, Brown University Library)*

## 105 – MILITARY MUSICIANS, C.1720

Six studies of mounted musicians by Martin Engelbrecht, a German engraver and print seller born in Augsburg on 16 September 1684 and died 18 January 1756. *(Image courtesy of the Anne SK Brown Military Collection, Brown University Library)*

## 106 – PFEIFER, 1600, TAMBOUR, 1700

A delightful study by Fritz Allemand of a flautist and drummer of the Austrian army. Frederick Alleman (better known as Fritz) was born at Hanau in 1812 and, after studying at the Vienna Academy, went on to establish himself as a popular military artist. He died in Vienna in 1866. *(Image courtesy of the Anne SK Brown Military Collection, Brown University Library)*

# 107 – TROMPETER. HEERPAUKER, 1700

From Fritz Allemand (see previous image), a trumpeter and percussionist of the Austrian army c1700. *(Image courtesy of the Anne SK Brown Military Collection, Brown University Library)*

# 108 – GRENADIER DRUMMER, GARDE IMPÉRIALE C.1870

Chromolith after Charles Escribe (1869-1914) showing a grenadier drummer of the French Imperial Guarde around 1870. The artist has provided an unusual view of the bottom head of the drum and its snares. *(Image courtesy of the Anne SK Brown Military Collection, Brown University Library)*

# 109 – ZOUAVE DRUM MAJOR AND MUSICIANS

His arm resting on his mace, the drum major looks casually to his left as he poses for French artist Jean Baptise Edouard Detaille. Born in Paris on 5 October 1848, Detaille died in 1912. The drum major and his drummers wear short, dark blue jackets with red braid and carry packs, rolled blankets, greatcoats and cooking pots on their backs ready for the march. *(Image courtesy of the Anne SK Brown Military Collection, Brown University Library)*

# SECTION TWO – SHEET MUSIC COVERS

## 110 – A MILITARY CHURCH PARADE

The cover features the artwork of Frank Wright who shows the drums and fifes of a guards or fusilier regiment led by a drum major. Written by James Ord Hume, the work was copyrighted in 1909 by Asherberg, Hopwood & Crew, Ltd of 16 Mortimer Street, London. *(Image courtesy of the Anne SK Brown Military Collection, Brown University Library)*

## 111 – THE SHAMROCK POLKA

The 1st Battalion Royal Irish Fusiliers had sailed from their station at Alexandria, Egypt on 24 September 1899 for South Africa. They arrived at Durban on 12 October and were at once moved up country towards Ladysmith. The 2nd Battalion was soon to join the 1st, sailing on the *Hawarden Castle* from England on 23 October and arriving at the Cape about 12 November. Both battalions were to see much action throughout the Second Boer War, and this was recalled as part of the design used by publisher Walter Whittingham for one of their sheet music covers—the 'Shamrock Polka' written by G Jervis Rubini. See the troops advancing up a steep slope under shellfire as the wounded are brought down by stretcher-bearers.

Featured in the artwork are three members of the Royal Irish Fusiliers, all of whom wear sprigs of shamrock in their caps. Following news of the severe losses suffered by the regiment during the fighting to relieve Ladysmith, Queen Victoria ordered that in future on St Patrick's Day all ranks should wear, as a distinction, a sprig of shamrock to commemorate the gallantry of her Irish soldiers during the war in South Africa. The image carries the initials 'MH' for Michael Hanhart. *(Image courtesy of the Anne SK Brown Military Collection, Brown University Library)*

## 112 – THE GALLANT GORDONS

To commemorate the action of the 1st Battalion Gordon Highlanders at the Dargai Heights, India on 20 October 1887, the London music firm of Francis, Day & Hunter published 'The Gallant Gordons', written by Albert Hall and composed by Orlando Powell. 'The Gordon Highlanders', records Sir William Lockhart in the 18 February edition of *The Broad Arrow*, 'went straight up the hill without check or hesitation. Headed by their pipers and led by Colonel Mathias…this splendid battalion marched across the open. It dashed through a murderous fire, and in forty minutes had won the heights, leaving three officers and thirty men killed or wounded on its way.' The sheet music cover illustrated was designed by Frank Dadd and shows one of the 'Gallant Gordons' being congratulated by two soldiers. One with green facings to his uniform

grasps firmly the palm of the Highlander, the other with white places a congratulatory hand on his shoulder. *(Image courtesy of the Anne SK Brown Military Collection, Brown University Library)*

## 113 – TOMMY ATKINS

For the sheet music cover of Brandon Thomas' composition 'Tommy Atkins', Frank Dadd features one of the Artists Rifles in his grey uniform. A rolled greatcoat can be seen slung across the body and the artist's initials are in the bottom right-hand corner of the image. This particular copy is from the Anne SK Brown Military Collection who also hold a letter from Brandon Thomas, dated London 1887, dedicating the song to a fellow comrade in the Artists' Rifles, one Private EV Salaman of 'F' Company. The full title of the regiment at the time was 20th Middlesex Rifle Volunteer Corps (Artists), its headquarters being in Duke's Road, Euston, London. As the name suggests, this part-time regiment was made up of painters, musicians, actors and others connected with the arts. *(Image courtesy of the Anne SK Brown Military Collection, Brown University Library)*

## 114 – THE RED MARINE

A marine sporting three good conduct stripes and in full marching order poses for the artist. Three of his mates, one of them hatless, stand chatting and an officer looks out from the hillside at a Victorian warship. The artwork for Brandon Thomas's 'The Red Marine' music sheet was supplied by Frank Dadd and had originally appeared in *The Graphic*. Published by J Bath of 23 Berners Street, London, there is a dedication at the top of the sheet to the wife of a Major-General Munro thanking her for the hospitality shown by the Royal Marines to the Artists Rifle Volunteers during a recent visit to Walmer. The Artists Rifles and another song by Brandon Thomas can be seen in the previous plate,

Frank Dadd was born in London on 28 March 1851 and studied painting at the Royal College of Art and the Royal Academy. As well as illustrating several books he worked regularly for the *Illustrated London News* and *The Graphic*. He died in 1929. *(Image courtesy of the Anne SK Brown Military Collection, Brown University Library)*

## 115 – SOLDIERS IN THE PARK

As a sheet music cover illustration for the 'Soldiers in the Park March' by Lionel Monckton, publisher Chappell & Co of 50 New Bond Street chose an image of the drums and fifes of the Grenadier Guards entertaining a London crowd as they leave Wellington Barracks for public duty close by Buckingham Palace. The music was copyrighted in 1898, the artwork by Lovig Edwards and the printing by the HG Banks Litho Company. London-born Lionel John Alexander Monckton (1861-1924) was the founder of the Oxford University Dramatic Society and, having given up practising law at Lincoln's Inn, went on to become Britain's most popular composer of Edwardian musical comedy.

## 116 – THE CADET CORPS GALOP

In a grey uniform piped with red, a young cadet salutes another boy who stands nonchalantly with his hands in his pockets. To the right, another raises his kepi cap to a young lady who wears a pink dress and has her hair held in place by a net. With a drummer in front, the parade looks on, as do the bonneted and top-hatted grown-ups behind. A pleasant countryside scene with a white mansion nestling behind trees on the slope of a hill: such is the cover of CW Smith's music to 'The Cadet Corps Galop', published in 1861 by Metzler & Co who could be found at 37, 38 and 35 Great Marlborough Street in London. The printer was Stannard & Dixon; the artist, his name just visible in the bottom left-hand-corner, was Robert Jacob Hamerton. Cadet companies had been formed and attached to volunteer corps from almost the very beginning of the Volunteer Movement in 1859 and were usually made up of thirty boys each. *(Image courtesy of the Anne SK Brown Military Collection, Brown University Library)*

## 117 – THE TRAMP GALOP

Just visible in the music cover to Charles Godfrey's 'The Celebrated Tramp Galop', is the signature F Sexton. The image shows the Scots Fusilier Guards on parade by a thatched cottage and church. Three young girls look on and a small dog seems to be barking at the officer leading the march. Charles Godfrey was the regiment's bandmaster, his publisher being Cramer & Co, Ltd of 201 Regent Street, London. The Scots Fusilier Guards were re-designated as Scots Guards in 1877. *(Image courtesy of the Anne SK Brown Military Collection, Brown University Library)*

## 118 – THE TRUMPET POLKA

Sheet music cover illustration for 'The Trumpet Polka' composed by Herrmann Koenig and published by Deacon of Market Street, Leicester. The image shows a trumpeter of the Royal Horse Guards. Visible in the bottom left-hand corner is the signature of the artist, John Brandard. Born 1812 in Birmingham, Brandard died in London on 15 December 1863 having been the designer of many hundreds of sheet music title pages. *(Image courtesy of the Anne SK Brown Military Collection, Brown University Library)*

## 119 – THE VOLUNTEER GALLOP

Colour lithographic music sheet cover by E Bates for 'The Volunteer Gallop', 'Composed and dedicated to the Gloucestershire Volunteers by Tewksbury Goodfellow (Gloucester City Rifles)'. Priced 2/6, the music was published 'In Aid Of The Gloucester City Rifle Company's Band Fund.'

In the City of Gloucester the 2nd Gloucestershire Rifle Volunteers Corps was formed as one company

at Gloucester Dock with the following officers, Captain William Vernon Guise, Lieutenant John Jones and Ensign Theodore Aylmer Preston. All three held commissions dated 21 October 1859. Also with headquarters at Gloucester Dock and of one company was the 3rd Corps with Captain Thomas De Winton, Lieutenant Henry Dowling and Ensign Richard T Smith. *(Image courtesy of the Anne SK Brown Military Collection, Brown University Library)*

## 120 – THE AWKWARD SQUAD

Sheet music cover to 'The Awkward Squad, Or the Experience Of A Volunteer Rifleman' by Henry Walker and published by Metzler & Co of 35, 37 & 38 Great Marlborough Street. The litho work was done by Thomas Packer, printing by Stannard & Dixon. With a tented camp in the background, a group of civilians and two cackling geese enjoying the spectacle as seven volunteer riflemen line up before a stout NCO. Tall, short, fat and strangers to military discipline, the 'awkward squad' look exactly that. Composer Henry Walker, a volunteer himself, dedicates his work to his comrades. *(Image courtesy of the Anne SK Brown Military Collection, Brown University Library)*

## 121 – THE DEVIL'S OWN WALTZ

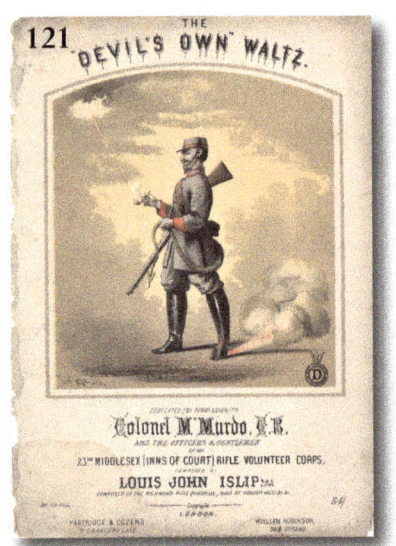

Sheet music cover for 'The Devil's Own Waltz' composed by Louis John Islip and published by Partridge & Cozens of 1 Chancery Lane, London. The artwork was by Thomas W Lee, the song dedicated to Colonel Montague McMurdo, CB and the officers and gentlemen of the 23rd Middlesex (Inns of Court) Rifle Volunteer Corps.

When King George III reviewed a volunteer corps composed of members of the legal profession, it was possibly his less-than-enjoyable experience with lawyers that caused him to refer to the troops as 'The Devil's Own'. After a lull in volunteer activity in Britain, 1859 once again saw civilians putting on uniform as a precaution against invasion and from the four Inns came the 23rd Middlesex Rifle Volunteer Corps. And here he is, the Devil himself, dressed in the grey and scarlet uniform of the 23rd, tail in hand, flames bursting from a hoofed foot, his pipe being ignited by lightning from the sky. In the bottom right corner of the image can be seen the letter D within a circle inscribed 'Painted not so black as he is'. Behind this, a three-pronged fork. *(Image courtesy of the Anne SK Brown Military Collection, Brown University Library)*

## 122 – THE PARIS BAND MARCH

The Tricolour flies high in the wind as His Imperial Majesty Napoleon III returns the salute of an officer during a march past of Zouaves. Mounted on a white horse, the French emperor holds his only child, Napoléon Eugène Louis Jean Joseph Bonaparte the Prince Imperial wearing a military uniform, in his lap.

Published by Brewer & Co, 'The Parish Band March' was composed by Stephen Glover and dedicated by him to the emperor. The art and litho work was by John Brandard (his signature visible in the bottom left hand corner of the image) and M & N Hanhart. John Brandard was born in Birmingham in 1812 and was for many years well known as an excellent lithographic artist and illustrator of sheet music covers. He died in 1863. *(Image courtesy of the Anne SK Brown Military Collection, Brown University Library)*

## 123 – WINCHESTER QUICK STEP

Surrounded by a border of green and red floral work is a single figure of an officer holding a sword. He is one of the Independent Company of Cadets commanded by Colonel William P Winchester.

The Independent Company of Cadets dates from 1741 and the formation that year of a volunteer company of young Boston gentlemen by Benjamin Pollard, its role to serve as a ceremonial bodyguard to the governors of Massachusetts. Pollard was one of Boston's leading citizens and sheriff of Suffolk County. By 1772 John Hancock, merchant, statesman and prominent patriot of the American Revolution, was commanding the corps, but due to friction between him and Governor Sir Thomas Gage, was dismissed. Unhappy with this, members of the corps took the decision to disband, turning in their Colours, uniforms and musical instruments to Hancock for safekeeping. The Independent Company of Cadets was, however, reformed sometime during 1776. The white uniform with red facings seen in the illustration was adopted in honour of a French regiment alongside which the cadets had served at Rhode Island in 1778.

The 'Winchester Quick Step' was composed by Adam Kurek, arranged by Thomas Comer and published by Charles H Keith of 67 & 69 Court Street, Boston. Thayer & Co, also of Boston, produced the litho work. *(Image courtesy of the Anne SK Brown Military Collection, Brown University Library)*

## 124 – THE KING'S COLONIALS IY MARCH

Here we have the original watercolour artwork prepared by artist W George for the cover of Archibald Evans' composition, 'The King's Colonials IY March', a work composed and dedicated to HRH The Prince of Wales in 1899. The captions have been roughly drawn and an instruction to the printer can be seen at the top right-hand corner.

In November 1901, a notice appeared in the *London Gazette* to the effect that His Majesty King Edward VII had been graciously pleased to approve the formation of a regiment of yeomanry to be composed of colonials resident in the County of London. The new unit was to be called the 4th County of London (The King's Colonials) Yeomanry, its four squadrons to be designated as: 'A' (British Asian), 'B' (British American), 'C' (Australasian) and 'D' (British African). The title of the regiment was in

1905, however, changed to the King's Colonials Imperial Yeomanry.

Artist W George shows a mounted trooper holding a rifle on his knee and wearing a slouch hat and ammunition bandolier. Badges are evident on both the headdress and collar, but these are unclear and their detail lacking. Individual squadrons wore their own distinctive insignia: an elephant for the British Asian Squadron, a beaver for the Americans and an ostrich for the South Africans. Two national emblems were adopted by 'C' Squadron which contained men from both Australia and New Zealand—a kangaroo and fern leaf. *(Image courtesy of the Anne SK Brown Military Collection, Brown University Library)*

## 125 – THE PIONEER'S QUICK STEP

Composed and arranged for the piano by James Monroe Deems, the cover of 'The Pioneer's Quick Step' shows, against a rural landscape with an encampment, a pioneer holding an axe and wearing a dark blue uniform with red collar and piping. His shako has two red bands, a tall, red-tipped dark plume and an eagle badge. Artist Lewis Towson Voigt has shown the jacket slightly open, revealing a white waistcoat with many buttons. The caption below the image tells how composer James Deems had dedicated his work to his friend James W Heron. The publisher was Samuel Carusi of Baltimore, the litho work and printing by Edward Weber & Co, also of Baltimore. A first page heading to the music, which is in Bb major and 2/4 time, tells how the work had been performed by the Independent Blues Band. The Anne SK Brown Military Collection notes that the subject featured is of the Baltimore Pioneers. *(Image courtesy of the Anne SK Brown Military Collection, Brown University Library)*

## 126 – SONGS IN LA FIGLIA DEL REGGIMENTO

*La Fille du Regiment* (The Daughter of the Regiment) was a comic opera in two acts by Gaetano Donizetti and first performed by the Paris Opéra-Comique at the Salle de la Bourse on 11 February 1840. In this sheet music version, published by C Holt Jr of 156 Fulton Street, New York, we see, with several French infantrymen and a drummer to keep her company, opera star Jenny Lind in the costume of a French cantinière. She holds her cap, with its red, white and blue rosette and red ribbon, in her left hand. The sheet was printed by Lewis & Brown of New York.

Born on 6 October 1820 in Sweden, Johanna Marie 'Jenny' Lind became known as the 'Swedish Nightingale'. She was one of the most highly regarded singers of the nineteenth century, performing all around the world including more than ninety concerts in the United States at the invitation of Phineas Taylor Barnum, the American showman, politician and businessman. Having settled in London, she was for a number of years a professor of singing at the Royal College of Music. *(Image courtesy of the Anne SK Brown Military Collection, Brown University Library)*

## 127 – JOLLY SONGS LANCERS

Charles Godfrey (1866-1935) was a bandmaster with the Royal Horse Guards and he is credited as the arranger in 1883 for 'Jolly Songs' Lancers published by Howard & Co of 25 Great Marlborough Street, London. The sheet music cover chosen shows a mounted officer of what appears to be the 12th Lancers. Certainly the red plastron and plume suggest this and, of course, the number 12 over the letter L below the crossed lances on the shabraque. But there seems to be a suggestion of a 17th Lancers type skull and crossbones device too. HC Maguire was responsible for the artwork, CB Court of 46 Poland Street, London, the litho work. *(Image courtesy of the Anne SK Brown Military Collection, Brown University Library)*

## 128 – THE DRYLAND SAILOR

You may remember him from his great hit, 'The Daring Young Man on the Flying Trapeze', or for the ever-popular song, 'Champagne Charlie.' George Leybourne, star of the British Victorian music hall had, if the music sheet cover illustrated is to be believed, the greatest success with 'The Dryland Sailor' published by Hopwood & Crew of 42 New Bond Street, London in 1860. A sad tale indeed, with the poor shipwrecked sailor, an arm and eye lost at sea, holding out his cap for some spare change. If his mournful face and obvious injuries do not move the passer by, then perhaps the very cause of his plight depicted on canvas might. Alfred Concanen the artist, Stannard & Dixon the printer. *(Image courtesy of the Anne SK Brown Military Collection, Brown University Library)*

## 129 – THE ROYAL HORSE ARTILLERY POLKA

'The Royal Horse Artillery Polka', written by Trumpet Major Henry Lawson and dedicated to Captain and Adjutant George Ashley Maude. Signed F Section, the artwork shows an officer with sword drawn galloping into action ahead of his battery. The publisher of the polka was Messrs Pask & Köenig of 441 Strand, London, a well-known musical instrument manufacturer and supplier to the army—Herman Köenig, the German cornetist and John Pask, the English flute maker. Henry Lawson has been noted as one of the best trumpeters of his day in the country, holding the position of principal trumpet with both the Royal Artillery Band and Royal Artillery Brass Band. He was appointed trumpet major of the Royal Horse Artillery Band in 1845. *(Image courtesy of the Anne SK Brown Military Collection, Brown University Library)*

## 130 – THE PRINCE ALBERT'S OWN OR THE ROYAL ELEVENTH HUSSARS

The 11th Light Dragoons had not long returned from India when in 1840, while stationed at Canterbury under the command of the Earl of Cardigan, the regiment had the honour of providing an escort to HRH Prince Albert of Saxe-Coburg and Gotha on the occasion of his marriage to his cousin Queen Victoria. It

then followed that the 11th Light Dragoons were formed into a hussar corps, the prince became colonel-in-chief, and a new title appeared in the Army List—the 11th Prince Albert's Own Hussars. *(Image courtesy of the Anne SK Brown Military Collection, Brown University Library)*

## 131 – THE GREY TOWER VALSE

The 'Grey Tower Valse' composed by Bandmaster H Carter of the Essex Artillery Volunteers. Litho by HC Maguire, printing by AB Court of 46 Poland Street, Soho, London. Volunteers are seen manning two guns on the lawn before an embattled country house. Fourteen gunners are present, one of them a young boy bugler.

Three individual artillery corps were formed in Essex during 1860-61 and these in 1880 were merged as the 1st Corps with headquarters at Stratford. Grey Towers was a mansion standing in eighty-five acres on the Hornchurch Road, Hornchurch, Essex, built in 1876 for Lieutenant-Colonel Henry Holmes, the owner of the Hornchurch Brewery. A deputy lieutenant for Essex, Colonel Holmes, served with the 1st Essex AVC. *(Image courtesy of the Anne SK Brown Military Collection, Brown University Library)*

## 132 – PARADE MARCH OF THE GREAT POTOMAC ARMY

In this example of Charles Fradel's march we have a fine portrait of Major-General George Brinton McClennan who during the American Civil War had played an important role in the formation and organisation of the Army of the Potomac. Two infantrymen are included in the image, one a Zouave wearing a blue jacket with red waistcoat and pantaloons. The litho work was done by Sherman & Hart of 99 Fulton Street, New York. *(Image courtesy of the Anne SK Brown Military Collection, Brown University Library)*

## 133 – INDIA'S REPLY

What better review for Francis, Day & Hunter's 'India's Reply' than that by 'Dagonet' of *The Referee* who had heard it sung by Leo Dryden at the Canterbury Music Hall. Known as 'The Kipling of the Halls', on dressed as an Indian Soldier had come the English music hall singer and comic to the '…thousands of spectators who sat packed like herrings in a barrel…cheered themselves horse.' There he is, dressed in red and about to draw his sword. Looking down, and flanked by images of India and Windsor Castle, is Queen Victoria. 'India's Reply' was written by John P Harrington to music by George Le Brunn. *(Image courtesy of the Anne SK Brown Military Collection, Brown University Library)*

## 134 – WHEN THE SUN GOES DOWN IN NORMANDIE

For the moment, all is quiet. Some dry and mud-free ground has been found, body-warming tents put up and uniform-drying fires lit. One soldier has drawn the short straw so, with rifle over his shoulder, he patrols the area on first watch. Three men enjoying the comforting flames sit around and chat. Or perhaps silence is preferred as each man reflects on the day. A day that has possibly seen much death and destruction far from home. This is Normandie, and the sun has gone down on another day of survival. In closed tents, others are thinking of home and writing letters.

Jeff Branen's lyrics take the form of a letter written by a soldier to his wife or sweetheart and they include: *When the sun goes down in Normandy / And the campfires are all a-glow / I'm dreaming of my lady love / Who's so far away across the waters / One of America's fairest daughters / Gee! Tonight I'm lonesome and blue / And gee! I know that you're lonesome too / When the sun goes down in Normandy / Then is when I sit and dream of you.* Music by Evans Lloyd, Publisher Jeff Braden of 145 West 45th Street, New York, artwork, Edward H Pfeiffer. (*Image courtesy of the Anne SK Brown Military Collection, Brown University Library*)

## 135 – THE MESSAGE THAT NEVER CAME

*Somewhere in old New England / Down a little country lane / A service star is gleaming / In a cottage through the windowpane / Tho' the postman passes daily / There's no knock upon the door / As day by day two fond hearts / For a message from a foreign shore / There's a message that's missing from over the foam / While two hearts are watching and waiting at home / One a sweetheart, and the other / Just a little gray haired mother / There's light in the window that gleams thru the night, / Though it beckons and beams all in vain / They will always keep the light a burning / For the message that never came.*

Albert Barbelle's artwork reflects the story told in the first verse of this 1918 song. Here is the postman who, for yet another day, has passed the cottage without stopping. The old mother looks disappointedly into the mailbox where, for over a year now, there has been nothing. 'Perhaps tomorrow', encourages a comforting arm, 'perhaps there will be some news tomorrow.' So back up the four steps that lead to the cottage, where the service star gleams in its window, the pair must go to their memories. Words and Music by Clayton Calhoun, publisher, Shapiro, Bernstein & Co of 224 West 47th Street, New York. (*Image courtesy of the Anne SK Brown Military Collection, Brown University Library*)

## 136 – THE MACDONALD MARCH

You may know him as 'Hector of the Battles' (or if you are a Gaelic speaker, '*Eachann nan Caith*') or even as the Highland soldier on the Camp Coffee bottles: Hector Archibald MacDonald. Born on a farm near

Dingwall in Ross-shire, he made his living in the manufacture of tartan and became a part time soldier with the 1st Invernshire Rifle Volunteers in March 1870. He liked military life so much that in the following year he enlisted as a regular with the 92nd Gordon Highlander at Fort George. Steadily he progressed through the ranks, gaining distinction for his bravery during the First Boer War in Egypt and at Omdurman. He was duly knighted in April 1901. But there would be scandal. Scandal so damaging that while staying at a hotel in Paris, where he learned from a newspaper that a court martial was imminent, he returned to his room and shot himself.

Here in the sheet music cover to Theo Bonheur's 'The MacDonald March', we see the hero in full dress uniform, his medals telling all that is needed to remember him. And hero he certainly was, the suicide of a war hero respected by all causing shock throughout Britain and the Empire. For his funeral, 30,000 turned up to pay their respects, many more from all over the world later visiting the grave. To this day Major-General Hector Archibald MacDonald remains a national hero in Scotland. The artwork for 'The MacDonald March' was produced from a photograph by Messrs FW Heath & Co. Theo Bonheur was a pseudonym of Charles Rawlings. *(Image courtesy of the Anne SK Brown Military Collection, Brown University Library)*

## 137 – THE ROYAL FUSILIERS MARCH

Francis, Day & Hunter's sheet music cover to George le Brunn's 'The Royal Fusiliers March' recalls the Battle of Inkerman in which the Royal Fusiliers (the 7th Regiment as it then was) took part in November 1854. The uniform of the regiment at the time is shown in the top left-hand corner along with that being worn at time of publication. The dedication at the top of the image refers to Lieutenant-Colonel Gardiner Frederick Guyon whose first commission in the army was dated 31 January 1865. He retired in August 1903 and died on 14 April 1924. The cover was designed by HG Banks of 60 Berwick Street, London. *(Image courtesy of the Anne SK Brown Military Collection, Brown University Library)*

## 138 – PARTANT POUR LA SYRIE

In the cover to '*Partant pour la Syrie*' (Leaving for Syria), artist and lithographer Augustus Butler has provided a superbly detailed image of an event held at Crystal Palace on 28 October 1854. Built to house the Great Exhibition of 1851 in Hyde Park and afterwards carried up to Penge Peak next to Sydenham Hill, Joseph Paxton's cast iron and plate glass by the Chance Brothers looks down on a vast crowd gathered around flags and trophies of arms to listen to a circle of French Guides perform. There in the centre is the bandmaster, the scarlet of his jacket concealed by thick gold lace, and all around with their swords hanging at their sides, his bandsmen play to a delighted audience who cheer and raise their hats in the air. *Partant pour la Syrie* was arranged by Charles Glover, violinist and musical director at the Queen's Theatre, and published by Addison & Hollier of 210 Regent Street, London. The printing was done by Stannard & Dixon. *(Image courtesy of the Anne SK Brown Military Collection, Brown University Library)*

## 139 – THE KING'S GUARD MARCH

Constructed on the site of a leper hospital by Henry VIII between 1531 and 1536, the royal palace of St James looks down in its red brick onto a crowded parade ground of 1854. With the hands of the clock above the north gatehouse just on eleven, guardsmen stand fast. Colours have been unfurled, their guardians deep in conversation, in a circle a band plays and, on the right, drummers await their orders. So is the scene used for the cover of 'The King's Guard', a prize-winning march of fifty years hence by JH Keith and published by Chappell & Co, Ltd. HG Banks was the printer. *(Image courtesy of the Anne SK Brown Military Collection, Brown University Library)*

## 140 – THE AFGHAN OR ALI MUSJID GALOP

The fortress of Ali Musjid stood at the narrowest point in the Khyber Pass since 1837 and would be the scene of the opening battle of the Second Anglo-Afghan War on 21 November 1878. In the sheet music cover for WH Westover's 'The Afghan or Ali Musjid Galop, we see British artillery firing as a long column of infantry move forward towards the Afghan defences. Published by E Griffith & Son of Birkenhead. *(Image courtesy of the Anne SK Brown Military Collection, Brown University Library)*

## 141 – THE IRISH LANCER POLKA

Composed by Charles Nicholson, the cover of 'The Irish Lancer Polka' features an officer leading a charge. With sword drawn he urges his men forward, the pennants of their lances and black lance-cap plumes flying in the breeze. The Anne SK Brown Military Collection date the work as 1904 which would place the colonel mentioned in the dedication as Lieutenant-General William Godfrey Dunham Massy, CB who was appointed in 1896 and served until succeeded by Thomas Arthur Cooke, CVO in 1906. *(Image courtesy of the Anne SK Brown Military Collection, Brown University Library)*

## 142 – A FAVOURITE SONG IN THE FARMER

An early illustrated song sheet published by Samuel William Fores on 5 November 1803. The year was to see Britain once again under threat of invasion from across the Channel, a fear that would see many thousands of civilians—businessmen, shopkeepers, bankers, clerks and farmers— throughout the land give up their spare time to train as soldiers. And here in this satire we see two of them. One proudly holds a representation of the Magna Carter secured to a staff reminiscent of a Roman fasces—that bundle of bound rods symbolizing authority and power. His friend gestures towards the flag as both men exclaim 'or united we'll die in the cause.' In six-eight time and the key of Eb Major, the verse recalls an earlier struggle in which British citizens were united: 'Shall a Corsican robber a Tyrant in France / Presume to give new laws'; Britain was having none of it.

Much in the words of the song has caught the attention of the artist. Here is the huge round oak with its entwined ivy and the mill that it shadows. Here too up the winding path is the ruined church and high in the sky, a parliament of rooks is about to descend on a tall pine. *(Image courtesy of the Anne SK Brown Military Collection, Brown University Library)*

## 143 – THE IRISH CAPTAIN

'The Irish Captain', written by HA Acton, arranged by Seymour Smith, published in London by John Blockley of 3 Argyll Street. A caricature of a British cavalry officer, Thomas Packer was the artist, William Spalding the lithographer. *(Image courtesy of the Anne SK Brown Military Collection, Brown University Library)*

## 144 – THE CHARGE OF THE 21ST

The chorus of JP Harrington, Fred Murray and Fred Leigh's 'The Charge of the 21st' refers to the regiment's involvement during the Crimean War. The artwork, however, depicts a scene during some later campaign. Copyrighted in the United States in 1898, the work was published in London by Francis, Day & Hunter of 142 Charing Cross Road and in America by TB Harms & Co, 18 East 22nd Street, New York. Slade Murray (1859-1913), was a popular music hall artist. *(Image courtesy of the Anne SK Brown Military Collection, Brown University Library)*

## 145 – THE LITTLE DRUMMER

Thomas Parker's artwork for 'The Little Drummer' shows a camp scene, the musician posing for the artist against a backdrop of tents, one flying the French flag, and two other soldiers. The song was written by George Linley, the music composed by Alphonse Leduc, the publisher in London, Robert Cocks & Co of New Burlington Street, the printer Stannard & Dixon. *(Image courtesy of the Anne SK Brown Military Collection, Brown University Library)*

## 146 – RIFLE CORPS QUADRILLES

The artist shows an un-named rifle volunteer corps during an exercise. All wear long, dark green coats, dark green trousers, black equipment and dark green flat caps. Composer William Henry Montgomery, artwork by J Brandard and the publisher was N & M Hanhart. *(Image courtesy of the Anne SK Brown Military Collection, Brown University Library)*

### 147 – RISING OF THE PEOPLE

Set sometime during the American Civil War, the scene on this sheet music cover features a blue-coated Union soldier just about to leave his Washington home for the front. By his side, an elderly white-haired man kneels so as to put a final adjustment to a bayonet frog. Behind him, a daughter holds a pack in readiness for her father's back, while another, younger this time, seems to be asking to be picked up. Her hand in his, a wife and mother makes the most of her husband's company while she can. All the family are here on this memorable day. Artwork by M Colburn.

### 148 – THE FIRST MANCHESTER VOLUNTEER RIFLE CORPS

Colour lithograph by Mansfield after C Black of a sergeant from the 6th Lancashire (1st Manchester) Rifle Volunteers Corps used on the music sheet cover of 'The First Manchester Volunteer Rifle Corps'. The publisher was R Andrews of 4 Oxford Street, Manchester.

The 6th was formed in Manchester on 25 August 1859 of twelve companies, a number of then being supplied by large Manchester firms such as Messrs JP and E Westhead, and Messrs J and N Phillips. For many years, the 6th occupied headquarters at Wolstenholm's Court, Market Street, Manchester and afterwards at 3 Stretford Road, Hulme. *(Image courtesy of the Ann SK Brown Military Collection, Brown University Library)*

### 149 – 1st MIDDLESEX VOLUNTEER ARTILLERY MARCH

Sheet music cover to the 1st Middlesex Volunteer Artillery March by CC Amos and 'Respectfully Dedicated To The Officers And Privates.' Published by CC Amos of 14 Craven Terrace, Hyde Park Gardens, London, the litho work was by Concanen & Lee, the printing by Stannard & Dixon. Three volunteers are featured wearing dark blue uniforms with scarlet collars, cuffs and piping. Three different forms of headdress are in evidence, a fur busby with scarlet bag (left), a blue field cap (centre) and a cocked hat with black feathers (right).

The 1st Middlesex Volunteer Artillery was formed on 16 July 1860, its first headquarters being recorded as No 70 Quadrant, Regent Street. A series of moves later followed with the corps ending up at Leicester Square by 1863. Disbandment came in 1876. *(Image courtesy of the Ann SK Brown Military Collection, Brown University Library)*

## 150 – BRISTOL VOLUNTEER MARCH

Included on the sheet music cover of the 'Bristol Volunteer March' are the words 'Composed and Inscribed To / Lieut. Colnl. Bush. Major Saville, / The Officers And Members Of The / Bristol Volunteer Corps.' The picture features two volunteers, one dressed in the blue uniform of a volunteer artilleryman, the other in the green of a rifle volunteer. The background shows other volunteers, some working large mortars.

The 1st Gloucestershire Artillery Volunteer Corps was formed at Bristol on 21 December 1859, the 1st Gloucestershire Rifle Volunteer Corps, commanded by Lieutenant-Colonel Robert Bush late of the 96th Foot, around the same time. The battalion had comprised ten companies by June 1860 and was permitted to include City of Bristol as part of its official title.

# BIBLIOGRAPHY

Army Museums Ogilby Trust, *Index to British Military Costume Prints 1500-1919,* 1972.

Regimental Histories, More than 250 consulted.

White, Arthur S White, *A Bibliography of Regimental Histories of the British Army,* The Naval & Military Press Ltd, 1992.

# A GUIDE TO MILITARY ART
# CHARLES HAMILTON SMITH'S
# COSTUME OF THE BRITISH EMPIRE

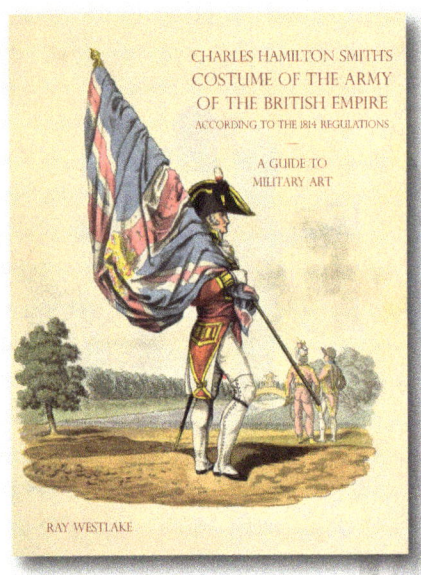

Reproduced here from a fine original volume is a full set of Charles Hamilton Smith's 60 plates. To accompany each plate, Ray Westlake has supplied additional explanatory notes.

Born on 26 December 1776 in East Flanders, then an Austrian province, Charles Hamilton Smith was a descendent of a Flemish Protestant family named Smet. In England he attended school in Richmond, Surrey, but having returned to Flanders he went on to study at the Austrian Academy for Artillery and Engineers at Malines and Louvain. He was a talented artist and as such provided one of the most valuable references to military costume ever produced.

In *Costume of the Army of the British Empire*, Hamilton Smith placed on record a detailed account of the several uniforms worn around the time of the Peninsular War. Originally issued in sets of four, the prints were produced from work drawn and etched by Hamilton Smith, then aquatinted by IC Stadler. Publication took place between March 1812 and June 1815 by the London firm of Colnaghi & Co who could be found in Cockspur Street. The printing was done by W Bulmer & Co of Cleveland Row.

In this *Guide*, Ray Westlake has drawn together a full set of Hamilton Smith's scarce and extremely difficult-to-find colour plates. As well as the British Army, a number of lesser-painted formations have been featured, such as the West India Regiment, King's German Legion, Duke of Brunswick Oels's Corps, the York Light Infantry Volunteers, Royal Military Asylum and native troops of the East India Company. For some 30 of them, he has included copies of Hamilton Smith's original drawings used for the work. Also useful are the six colour charts showing facing and lace colours. With a total of 60 informative plates, this *Guide* will prove to be a welcome addition to the library of all those interested in military uniform.

**Hard & Softback Editions: 126 pages complete with 60 full page costume plates**
**Product code: 30247 Softback Published at £30**
**Product code: 30247HB Hardback Published at £45**
www.naval-military-press.com

# A GUIDE TO MILITARY ART
# ROWLANDSON'S LOYAL LONDON VOLUNTEERS
*Rowlandson pictures each individual in a particular named drill position.*

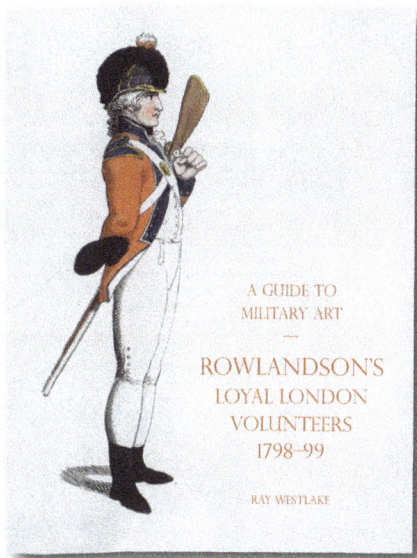

Reproduced here from a fine original volume is a full set of Rowlandson's 87 plates, together with an additional two that were to be included in some (even scarcer) bound volumes by the publisher. To accompany each plate, Ackermann prepared a page of letterpress which included details of when the corps had been formed, its uniform and names of officers. That text has been reproduced here in full, together with additional notes prepared by Ray Westlake.

In this volume are presented some of Thomas Rowlandson's most elegant and effective works in terms of pure printmaking. The result is arguably the greatest of all military costume books, in that it ascends beyond being a mere record of uniforms to become an important social document and a cohesive work of art, all produced at a time of great national peril.

The phenomenon of the volunteer corps arose as a response to the perceived imminent danger of invasion by the French Napoleonic forces.

Rudolph Ackermann notes in his introduction that "At this moment, the enemy had advanced their best regulated legions to the shores of the British Channel; and for the determined purpose of spreading through our land such miseries as have already rendered wretched their own".

The British response was immediate and defiant, and Ackermann goes on to note that when the Loyal Volunteers of London were inspected by the King on 21st June 1799 the roll-call of volunteers, manning 11 different positions, totalled just over 12,200 men.

The present work serves as a record of that overwhelming show of loyalty, as well as of the uniforms of all the main volunteer forces.

Importantly, Rowlandson pictures each individual in a particular drill position, the name and details of which are given in the engraved text beneath each figure.

The most original set of English military plates from the Napoleonic period – The Loyal Volunteers of London & Environs, Infantry & Cavalry, in their respective uniforms. Representing the whole of the Manual, Platoon & Funeral Exercise in 89 plates. Designed and etched by T. Rowlandson and originally published in London during 1798-99 by Ackermann. Dimensions: 21.59 x 27.99 cm.

**Hard & Softback Editions: 198 pages complete with 89 full page colour uniform plates**
**Product code: 25867 Softback Published at £30**
**Product code: 25867HB Hardback Published at £45**

www.naval-military-press.com